"If you are among the millions of people on this planet searching for a simple way to enrich your life, hoping to find that one revelation which could open your mind to a whole new understanding of the universe, then *Ghost Mind* by Gregory Rhoades is a book you should read. Skillfully crafted, Gregory's true story on exploring the depths of consciousness through powerful meditation could easily become the script for a wonderful movie. I loved reading *Ghost Mind* and highly recommend it to everyone."

Paul Elder – Author of *Eyes of an Angel*

GHOST MIND

Misadventures & Epiphanies

PART I
A MIDNIGHT MEMOIR

By

G. M. Rhoades

Mountain Valley River Publishing

Disclaimer for **Ghost Mind, A Midnight Memoir**

The author has done his best to protect the privacy of any individuals involved within this story, some names have been changed, some have given verbal permission for their inclusion in this book, but all stories are based on events that actually happened. Much care was taken to ensure accuracy at the time of publication. The author disclaims any liability for recreated dialogue for the sake of writing this memoir. While some details have been modified, the story remains true to actual events based on the life of the author. All opinions are the authors and all events are retold as truthfully as he can remember.

Published by Mountain Valley River Publishing

Cover Photos by: Michelle Halpern
Edited by: Thomas Horner & Avinash Marathe
Special Thanks: Denise Lawson & Chiwha Slater
ISBN: 979-8-9904968-0-4

A LOOK WITHIN

PREFACE

The book you hold in your hands is what I call a midnight memoir. Conventional critics might call it something else. It is a subgenre of stories told by people like me who have struggled with mental illness and overcame it.

We were willing, even desperate to try something new, unfamiliar and genuine. We looked hard to see through the folly of our ways, and through honest painful self-introspection eventually came to lay bare the root cause behind agonizing tribulations, ceaseless torment and mystifying despair.

Those of us whose brains are on fire are not isolated from the world. We're an inherent part and result of the current ills that plague our society. This needs a long hard look—I hope this book might provide a new perspective of possibility for those who still endure depression, and who feel lost or alone.

When I reached the point of no return, where death seemed inevitable, I managed to heal my broken mind and come out the other end. I read deeply into psychology, life after death, various religious and spiritual traditions, and tried meditation, and basically was looking for anything that could really make the difference in my life. The road I followed lead me back in the general direction of sanity, but along the journey I was filled with uncertainty.

I've warned and tried to help some friends teetering on that knife's edge of mental illness, only to watch them vanish down an invisible trap door of mental torment themselves. In a way, my compassion for them has inspired me to scribble down this tale of how during my own darkest hour—when I liked myself better while I was sleeping—an enlightening idea opened up new opportunities I couldn't even dream of. This idea made perfect sense: *If I could find God, all of my feelings of self-hatred would vanish.* I wasn't interested in blind faith, mere belief or a fairytale quest. If I could realize the presence of the divine within myself, practically speaking, I might be able to find my way out of the sludge I was currently sinking in.

Imagine your life was just a dream. Within this dream you've forgotten who you are, and must remain in this delusion for the rest of your life. What if the dream became a nightmare? If you had the choice, would you try to wake up? If life is just a dream, and waking up meant finding what some call enlightenment, then was are the practical steps involved in this process. I wanted to find out. Luckily for me, enlightenment wasn't rocket science.

The experiences noted in my misadventures really did actually happen. I called my friends to tell them about my book, and asked if they'd okay if I used their real names in my story. Out of respect I've kept a few of their identities hidden. Also, I've had to condense some timelines, combine similar characters and alter the sequence of some events slightly for the sake of the story.

There are many experiences in life that wouldn't be interesting in a book, so I chose to follow the theme of meditation. I've had many experiences related to this topic and although many of my experiences are supernatural in nature, they're all true. I hope my story will maybe help a few people out there who are looking to uncover a deeper meaning to their lives or are stuck thinking life is a pointless trap. That's how I felt. I wanted to escape this matrix.

Let's say life was a blank canvas, and you could paint anything at all, would any of you decide to stop painting and instead seek out the person who made the canvas? If only it were as simple as the movie the Matrix, and all you had to do was choose the red pill, waking up wouldn't be so difficult. But perhaps the choice itself is the red pill. Because without choosing to wake up, we'd remain asleep.

CHAPTER I

OUT OF THE BLUE

"The day my mother told me she could fly was the day my world changed forever."

Slumped in the passenger seat of my mother's car, I kept staring out the window, daydreaming, lost in the spectacle before my eyes. I was twelve years old. We were on our way home from one of my acting auditions.

The late afternoon sun had turned Miami into a timeless painting of colorful buildings, endless rows of palm trees, toll bridges, water, and clouds. I particularly liked the clouds that day because they were billowing towers of white graced with dramatic orange hue. It's a fact that sunsets in south Florida are more spectacular than almost any other place on earth, and when I was a kid, they often seemed otherworldly.

My mother leaned over to me and got my attention. "I had an out-of-body experience once. Did you know that?" She spoke as if it was a confession to me.

Something went off in my head.

I sat upright, as if I had just awakened. "What do you mean? What's that?"

"My soul left my body," my mom said, simply. "I separated from my body and could fly around."

"You could fly around? What like superwoman?"

"Anyone can fly around, if you have an out-of-body experience."

My brain felt like it had just been set on fire. I repeated the unfamiliar phrase, "out-of-body experience," trying to memorize the words.

Maybe my mother's Cherokee Native American heritage had something to do with this, I thought, though I really I didn't know what she was talking about.

Besides being a great mom, Susan was my chauffeur, my agent, and a stage mom who knew how to work the advertising scene so well that I had landed five top agencies in South Beach in a remarkably short period of time. As a child, I worked print, runway, commercial modeling, and acting jobs. There was even an article published about me about being a new hot talent on the Miami scene.

One job I did was for George Lucas. He produced a Super Mario Bros. 3 video game commercial. You can see it now on YouTube. I was in the crowd wearing blue sweats like the kid standing next to me. The producers had picked him up off the street that day, and maybe because he was a Johnny Depp lookalike, they focused on him instead even though I was hired as the principle talent. They cut me into a close up twice, dressed in blue and then white, chanting along with all the other kids, "Mario, Mario, Mario!"

The camera, on a helicopter, pulled away from us, all dressed in blue again, until dozens, hundreds, then thousands of kids could be seen shouting the name of the famous video game plumber. The view kept expanding until, in special effect animation, the curvature of the world was visible, with millions of kids spilled across the continent to form a picture of Mario's face. A narrator provided the closing words: "He's back. All you had to do was ask."

I made $12,000 from that ad alone. The kid they picked up off the street only got $700. I held no hard feelings because I didn't really want to be there anyway.

My mother drove me around the city like I was a prince and I felt like one too. Super Mario paid the most money I ever made from an ad. I would usually bring in $75 an hour for most jobs. Not bad for a kid.

I don't recall what she might have been saying before announcing her out-of-body experiences. I just remember we were on the way back to our apartment in Surfside. We saw lots of water outside the window, either canals, the ocean or the bay. Miami is actually a bunch of islands strung together by bridges: small ones, big ones, arched and flat bridges, even drawbridges. I hated waiting for drawbridges. They were the worst. At my age, I had no patience to wait for them to lift it up, to wait for the boat to sail by, and to wait for them to lower it back down. It took forever.

The wind blew into the open window and through my hair as I stared at the water. I had wanted to be home already, sitting in front of the TV while my mom made dinner. But she had snapped me out of it, out of the blue, with her out of the body story that would alter my life forever.

"When did this happen?" I asked.

"Well, it first happened when I was in college."

"It happened more than once?" I was shocked.

Finally, finally, finally we had something to talk about! My mother and I never spoke much, which might sound strange, and I didn't understand it myself. For my age, I might have acted super confidant, but beneath my smile, I was afraid. I didn't really know why.

At the time, I hated talking to my mother. Whenever she asked me how my day was, I felt frustrated. It would take years for me to realize I had lots of bottled-up emotions that I never felt safe to express—from my parents' divorce, my own insecurities, all sorts of issues.

The closest I might come to explaining?

I was like a deer in the headlights of an oncoming truck, and I was terrified that the truck wouldn't stop, but I was doing nothing to stop it or get out of its way. Instead, I kept smiling and the truck kept coming.

In my mind, there wasn't anything I could do.

That's how I usually felt when I tried to talk to my mother, but at this moment, I forgot about the sunset and the water and I gave her my full attention. Spellbound, this was something I wanted to talk about.

"Tell me what happened," I said firmly.

"Well, let me remember." She smiled. "It happened so long ago. I was living on campus at Purdue University—that's in Indiana—and I was studying for exams. I was up late and I kept falling asleep, so I bought a coffee. I must have had three or four more cups, but the caffeine didn't help. I couldn't stop myself from falling asleep, and I kept telling myself, 'You have to stay awake.'

"That's when it happened. Suddenly, I just shot out of my body."

"Really?" I said, skeptical again. "You shot out of your body. Just like that?"

"Yeah, down the hall. I shot out like a bullet from a gun. Like I was flying super-fast."

"Wait, wait." I felt like I was missing something. "Start from the beginning. Tell everything."

"Well, let's see." My mother considered the details. "I studied at a table in this long hallway. I had a pile of books with me because it was finals week, and I wanted a good grade, so I kept going over the material until after midnight. No matter what I did, though, I couldn't stop myself from falling asleep, and when I did fall asleep, I shot out of my body lightning-fast down the hall. I was flying so fast I couldn't stop myself. I thought, 'I'm going to hit those doors.' But then I flew right through them and rocketed outside. I soared into the sky and I could see the Moon. Then I began flying fast toward the Moon and I heard a voice say, 'She's coming!'"

"'She's coming,'" I repeated. "Who said that?"

"I don't know."

"And then what happened?"

"I got scared when I heard the voice. I didn't know who was speaking and I was terrified that I was flying too high. I shot back into my body and opened my eyes."

I sat back in the passenger seat.

"That's it?"

"Yeah, that's all that happened."

I felt let down that the story had ended. I wanted to hear more.

"Did it ever happen again?"

"Yes, it did."

"It did? I want to hear about that, too."

"Geez, you really like this story," my mom said, laughing.

By this point, we had arrived home. My mother pulled into the driveway to the apartment complex on Bay Harbor Island, but I wasn't ready for our conversation to end. She seemed surprised I was that interested in this topic. She said she needed to make dinner first, so I should shower and then change clothes.

After I watched half an hour of TV, we sat down for dinner, and I asked her again to tell me more.

"I used to have so many experiences," she said. "I should have written them down."

"Why didn't you?"

I felt annoyed and frustrated, as if her lack of care for detail was on purpose and meant to spite me. Neither she nor I had any idea how much this conversation would motivate me to have an out of body experience of my own.

"I didn't, because I used to think I was going crazy," she said. "I went to see doctors about it because it happened so frequently. I couldn't stop it, and no one seemed to understand what it meant. Then I found this book by Robert Monroe that answered all my questions. I was having out-of-body experiences."

Robert Monroe.

It was the first time I had ever heard his name, and while I had no idea who this person was, I was determined to investigate further. In the moment, though, I remained silent while eating my vegetables and patiently waiting to hear another out-of-body story.

"Ah, yes, there was one when I was living with your father," my mother said, at last. "I was falling asleep and I recognized this terrible sensation. It felt like a train running right through our apartment and the entire room was shaking. For some reason, I could control the experience after these, um… vibrations. I would roll over and lift myself out of my body. I remember looking up. There was a heavy dark cloud right above me. I started meditating and the cloud got smaller and smaller, and then it just disappeared."

"That's a cool one," I said. "So, you could control these… experiences?"

"Yes. And I would have them frequently. Almost every night."

"That's amazing," I said. I chewed my dinner quickly, trying to rush through the last of the vegetables because I hated them so much. My mom's cooking was very bland.

My mother was a beautiful woman and, although you don't notice these sorts of things as a kid, I even then knew that she walked with grace and had a peaceful aura. She was like an angel. She never raised her voice at me once. When she smiled it always made me want to smile, too. I could tell she was enjoying the fact that we had finally found something in which we were both interested.

"Tell me more," I said.

She laughed. "I'm sorry, I can't remember any more. This all happened so many years ago."

Our talk had ignited something in me. Was it really possible to leave your body? As a twelve-year-old I could barely understand the concept, but I found it so amazing that I wanted to know all the details. After dinner, my mom went to a shelf and handed me a book written by Robert Monroe. I had just finished reading a science fiction book about a kid being trained to fight a war in space, and, as it turned out that was the last book of fiction I would read during my teenage years.

Robert Monroe was born in 1915 and died in 1995. He was a radio broadcasting executive, but was more well known for founding The Monroe Institute, an organization that examined the idea of altered consciousness. It was his 1971 book, *Journeys Out of the Body*, which gave the world the term "Out-of-Body Experience, or "OBE."

After I finished reading his book, I was not only convinced that there was life beyond death, but I was also terrified of where I might end up after I died.

In the Astral Plane, Monroe had traveled to hellish landscapes where souls suffered despair and great sadness. He had to fight dark entities for hours, entities that were trying to take over his soul, and he had wandered in what seemed like an abyss with only darkness as an ever-present companion.

The world people went to after death seemed like a dangerous place, a place I needed to know more about. I became obsessed. I had to know: where would I go after death?

I returned to my mother's bookshelves for more literature about the afterlife. I read every book related to the topic I could find. Slowly, I began building a road map of "The Beyond" in my head. In all of these books, there were definite patterns and different levels you could reach—

higher levels that resembled celestial heavens and lower levels that resembled ghost worlds. In my mind, the question became, how do I get to the celestial levels? And then an opposite question, equally important to me, arose: how do I avoid the creepy dark lower worlds? At this point I didn't know.

These twelve-year-old thoughts made *life* seem like a nightmarish video game that I had no choice but to play, and a game in which every player died.

In my mind, your role in life was like being an actor on a reality TV show called *Death Island*. "Welcome to the Island of Death," the host would say. "You're free to enter, but once you do, you can never leave."

I imagined everyone else bustling on board the boat, except for me. I would stop and question the host.

"Did I hear you correctly? Everyone who joins this show dies?"

And the host would offer a casual smile. "Oh, don't worry. Everyone does it."

That idea sunk into my head. Imagine... everyone else was fine with the premise of the show. Everyone, except for me. For me, dying was an appalling idea: *What do you mean I can't go back to the world of the living after I die? What is death, anyway? Is it really a permanent sort of thing? If I'm going to die no matter what, then what's the point of being alive?* I didn't know the answers to any of these questions, but I was determined to find out.

In the meantime, I also developed a passion for sales. As a child model I would just stand still, smile and make money. I hated that job. And although I was also making up to $700 per commercial, I was doing mostly boring print work. So, in elementary school, I decided to start my own candy business. I didn't tell teachers about this, but between classes, I'd sell my candy to other students out of my backpack. The most popular candy was this bright red lollipop on a ring that you could wear as jewelry. I'd slip it on my middle finger and flash it around campus and stuff coins into my pocket. It was very difficult not to eat the candy myself but I didn't want to eat my profits.

After school, my mom would drive me to my acting auditions. This routine went on for several weeks and after several weeks of finally selling out of candy, I calculated my profit while sitting in the car next to my mother. My mother asked why I looked so sad. I explained that the profit I made was less than ten dollars. That's when I told my mom I was going to quit the candy business. No more ring pops for me. But she encouraged me, saying that I was not only a good actor, but also a good salesman. She wanted to cheer me up so she let me borrow the cassette tapes she had ordered from the Monroe Institute.

"These tapes are meant for adults," she said. "But you can try them out. Just be careful."

"Will they help me to have an out of body experience?"

"Possibly," she smiled. "It is a very special program."

"What will it be like?" I asked.

"Impossible to say. You're gonna have to try it for yourself," my mom said reassuringly. "Magic might happen."

If my mother could leave her body at will, what other impossible things might be true? That night, I lay in bed, staring at the glow in the dark stars on my ceiling. My mind raced, replaying my mother's story and the stories of Robert Monroe over and over. One questions remained. How did they do it? How can I have an O.B.E. experience?

I got my head set out and played the tape. As I closed my eyes, trying to imagine what it would feel like to suddenly leave my body. Would it hurt? Would I also be able to fly? I pictured myself floating above my bed, looking down at my body.

I lay still for an hour but the experience never came. As I finally drifted off to sleep, one thought echoed in my mind: *nothing would ever be the same again.*

CHAPTER II

A MONK'S PURGATORY

After my obsession with the afterlife began, my mother asked, "Would you mind going to live with your father?"

"Sure," I said.

I knew she had a hard time as a single mother. My sister was only one year old and I was twelve. My mom's life would become simpler and easier without me around. So, I left her house in Miami Beach and moved in with my father. He lived 15 minutes inland in a two-bedroom duplex in Biscayne Park.

Living with my father was a drastic change that I was not at all prepared for. My mom had failed to tell me anything about my father's volatile personality. When I was little, my mother was one of the nicest, sweetest people you'd ever meet. Everyone thought she was an angel sent from Heaven, and maybe she was. As I grew, I began to realize that she preferred to sweep her feelings under the rug. She wouldn't talk about the difficult stuff. Well, I really wish she hadn't suppressed her feelings about my father's brutal rage. If we had talked about it I could have made a more informed decision, or at least been ready for him, if that was possible.

Inside the privacy of our home, I could tell my mom felt lost in the world. She had never really overcome the scars of a traumatic childhood, brought on by her alcoholic parents who fought all the time. I found out later that was why she kept me away from her side of the family — they were all alcoholics, even my uncles and aunts. Aunt Lisa was the worst. She howled at my mom late into the night on the phone, always demanding attention and blaming Susan, my mom, for nothing in particular, as far as I could tell. My mom was a saint and what Lisa was mad about, I will never know. At the time I didn't realize that Lisa was a drunk, only calling my mom at midnight.

Later in life, my dear sweet mother confided in me that she had often wished she could leave this earth early and fly up to Heaven. Happiness eluded her in this life. Susan's days were filled with pain and grief, though she never told a soul. No one could have guessed how much pain she was actually struggling with. Perhaps that's why she dropped out of Purdue University and moved into an Indian Guru's commune where she met my dad, seeking an escape.

My dad on the other hand, didn't care about putting up a false front. He was stoic by nature, a military man with a strong work ethic. My father could be an angry bull, but I respected him. That was one of the reasons why I never wanted to move back to my mom's house. I desperately needed to connect to my mom, but she was too wrapped up in her own struggles as a single mother.

My mental well being was on edge. When I failed to wash my breakfast dishes before going to school one day, he flew into a rage, punched a hole in my door, raised his voice and kicked the wooden coffee table across the room — an act that once broke his toe. I just sat there quietly and said nothing like a mute. So when he broke his toe, I didn't feel bad, instead I felt the satisfaction of knowing justice was served. I don't know why I didn't mention any of this to my mother. I was too young to know better. Despite his emotional volatility, I was curious why at other times his aura radiated with a peaceful, calm energy that expressed a mystical quality of wisdom to me. I didn't know it at the time, but he was extremely gifted at meditation.

He and I didn't talk much at first. He never punched me or physically hurt me. I think because his own father beat him he held back on me. He told me a story about when he was an eight-year-old boy, his father kicked him across the room for no reason, leaving him with scars that his mother didn't know what to do with. He moved out of the house when he was only 16. He had no one to look up to until he found his Guru and applied himself diligently to his spiritual practice. He was also good at was telling stories.

Despite his own depression, he didn't turn to alcohol. He sought to heal himself through meditation. I loved him because he was my father, but I never called him dad. It perhaps was the only thing a child could do to show him I didn't approve of his behavior.

During that time, I became more focused on acting, since I had been accepted at Norland Middle School of the Performing Arts. The majority of the student population was either African American or Hispanic. It was a magnet school in the inner city. Though I was bused in, my mom still picked me up after school and drove me to my auditions and modeling jobs.

In our travels she would stop at a health food store, next to which was a spiritual or "new age" kind of a bookstore called *The Unicorn*. My mom agreed to let me go in the bookstore when she shopped for the groceries. Still fascinated about life after death, reading book after book on the subject, I was delighted by what I found inside the shop.

One day, after walking around looking at crystals and little Buddha statues, I made my way to the bubbly bookstore clerk at the counter. She might have been in her early twenties or younger. She was cute. I asked if she had any books about out-of-body experiences or life after death.

The clerk smiled, led me into a section of the store labeled "Astral Projection," and handed me a book from the shelf.

"This is a good one," she said.

I leafed through the pages, noticing that she seemed interested herself.

"Have you ever had an out-of-body experience?" I raised an eyebrow, my eyes flickering with excitement.

The clerk had wavy brown hair, and I liked the way her lips curled when she smiled. Those lips were luscious and plump with red lipstick. I was starting to notice these sorts of things.

She lit up and nodded, her cheeks turning a rosy pink.

I perked up. "Would you mind telling me about it?"

"Well," she stalled, and then decided to go ahead. "I was at a party with my friends doing some things I shouldn't have been doing. That's what happens at these sorts of parties."

I didn't ask the questions that jumped into my head about "these sorts of parties." What did she mean by that? What shouldn't she have been doing?

"Well, anyway," the clerk said, "I got a ride home and after I lay down in bed, I fell asleep. Or, at least, I thought I fell asleep, because I realized I couldn't move my body. I was stuck or my body was stuck. I tried to wiggle my fingers and I couldn't feel them! But that's not the strange thing."

My eyes widened. "No?"

"The strange thing was my eyes. They were open. I was looking around my bed thinking I must have what's called sleep paralysis. That's where you can't move your body at all."

"Wow, sounds scary."

"That's nothing," she said. "It's also what happens right before you have an out-of-body experience. So, I was looking into the spirit world."

My unasked questions multiplied quickly: how long did this sleep paralysis thing last? What did the spirit world look like? What did she even mean by the words, *spirit world*?

The clerk continued. "What really, totally freaked me out was that even though I couldn't move, I could still look around my room."

"So your eyes were open?" I asked.

"No, my eyes were closed. I was looking into the spiritual world with my spiritual eye."

"Spiritual eye?" I repeated, curious. "So, did you see any spirits?"

"Yes. There was something or someone standing at the end of my bed."

"Something? What was it?"

"I don't know. But when I looked down, this thing was looking at me in a peculiar sort of way. He had a crazy big smile, from ear to ear. This little dark spirit standing at the foot of my bed was just looking at me and grinning. It was an evil sort of grin, too. He was wearing a hood that covered his eyes, so he didn't look human. He was kind of ghoulish, like out of a horror film. So, I freaked out, and then, when I woke up the next day, I swore I'd never do what I did at that party again."

"What'd you do at the party?" I couldn't help myself. I had to know.

"You're a bit young for me to tell you. But just know that it was bad."

I took a guess in my head, and I imagined she must have done drugs. I was a little in shock. At this point in my life that was easily the scariest story I had ever heard.

Entities were real?!

As impossible as it seemed, that was what the clerk said: she had seen a short dark entity, one with malicious intent. It wanted something from her and wasn't leaving her alone. The afterlife seemed like a place filled with creatures that wanted to possess your soul or something. I was bewildered by what I'd heard.

"Thanks for telling me your story," I said, finally, feeling troubled.

"Come back and talk to me anytime you like," she said.

The clerk gave me the sweetest smile I'd ever seen and then bounced on back to the cash register.

I browsed more bookshelves and came across a book about a Catholic monk who lived in a monastery his whole life, but when he died, he went to Hell. Well it wasn't an actual Hell like one we'd imagine but someplace like it. So much for living a good life dedicated to spiritual righteousness. Even that wouldn't save you! I bought the book.

Over the next two weeks, before I went to bed, I read about the monk. The thing that made the biggest impression on me, was that after he died, the monk went to an astral sub-hell, a little town where everyone looked normal, except they were all acting rude, agitated, and frustrated, as if they were massively pissed off with each other and everything around them. No one was happy or in a good mood or nice to each other at all. The story seemed way too vivid, and real, as if it had actually happened, and that scared me. What if I ended up going to a place like that after I died? I shuddered.

Feeling out of place, the monk left the small village and wandered down the road. He traveled back to the field of grass where he had first arrived. Looking around, he saw no one. He dropped down on his knees and looked up into the blue sky with his palms clasped together. He prayed! It was difficult to see at first but something slowly appeared to be floating above him. A soft light maybe? It was hard for the monk to make it out at first, but as he kept praying, the angel materialized into a body made of pure light and asked him if he'd like to go to a better place. He readily agreed. The Angel reached out and took the monk's hand in his, and soon they were flying.

This better place where he was taken seemed more like a school in a city, where he was to be educated about the afterlife. This didn't seem like Heaven to me. In the school, the monk had to review his life and it all seemed very mundane. Even more disturbing to my thirteen-year-old mind—everyone had jobs! People had to work after they died?! Come on, now. Why did these souls need to work if they didn't need food or clothing? Everybody had a damn job! This was insanity. I didn't like this Heaven much more than Hell. What was Heaven after all? Is there even a Heaven?

This whole Heaven thing was becoming a bigger worry by the minute.

Later in the book, a teacher in this heaven-like city died right in front of the monk. The teacher's body transformed into a body of light. Maybe the teacher had passed a test and moved on to a higher stage in his light body. He just vanished and there was no mention of where the teacher actually went. I found that disturbing.

The stupid monk had no idea about what was happening. He was trapped going to school and had no spiritual understanding whatsoever. He had wasted his life being a monk! He had ended up in hell after all, because he was a self-righteous angry fool.

The story woke me up to something though. In the afterlife—and maybe in this world—like attracts like. This appeared to be especially true in the afterlife. The various levels of hells and heavens must have some kind of spiritual magnetism attracting us. After we die, I reasoned, we are automatically pulled to the level we have reached here on Earth.

"Well," I thought to myself. "I'm figuring this stuff out after all."

My mother and father first met while living at a meditation center in Washington D.C. The place was kind of like a monastery, or rather, it was supposed to be. My parents clearly violated the rules, because my mother became pregnant and they had to move out and get an apartment.

When I was three, when my parents were about to separate, they asked me whom I wanted to live with. I just said "mom." I didn't know, that was all I could say. The terror I felt chilled me to the bone. I was scared of my father from that moment on. For most of my childhood, I lived with my mom. It wouldn't be until I was 12 that I learned what it was like to live with my dad.

My father thought of himself as a serious artist. He dreamed of becoming famous and hung his Art Deco paintings all over the apartment. He had no idea how his mood swings were turning a confidant kid into an insecure one. However, I don't want to give the impression that he was all bad. The harder memories tend to stick, sting and stand out more. Sure, he got angry, but he wasn't upset all the time. Most of the time he turned out to be quite peaceful. But he was a quiet man who liked solitude.

He took me to the movies, bought me comic books, and taught me how to play chess. At first, I wasn't good at it, but he reminded me that chess was all in how well you could focus. Slowly, I began to see how it worked. I focused on all the possible moves. I could see two or three moves ahead. I began to understand how to think things through and predict the future. Eventually, I was good enough to win. I could keep a poker face, so he wouldn't know that I had a devastating attack figured out. These were some of my fonder memories.

In his more meditative, peaceful moods, he proved to be quite a smart man. He was talented at interpreting dreams, and taught me something about how to do it after analyzing one of my more vivid ones.

One day at breakfast, I said, "I was standing on the ground floor inside a castle tower. A stairwell spiraled upward along the stone walls and when I looked up, it seemed like the tower went on forever."

"There was an old wooden elevator attached to a rope in the center of this tower, and inside the elevator car, an old wise man spoke to a boy about my age. I wanted desperately to be the boy the wizard was talking to. Instead, I was the boy standing off to the side.

"The elevator began rising. They were leaving.

"I ran up the spiral staircase in order to keep up with them, but the stone steps were wet and slippery. There was no railing to keep me from falling, and soon, I was aware of how high I was climbing. The slick steps narrowed. Keeping pace with the elevator was increasingly difficult. I didn't want to lose the old man and the boy, but I also didn't want to fall.

"Then, of course, I fell.

"When I looked up again, I was disheartened to find I hadn't landed on the ground floor. Instead, I had plummeted about 15 steps *below* the ground floor.

"I now stood in a hallway.

"I climbed the 15 steps just to get back to the platform where I had originally started in order to begin again. Each time I climbed the stairs, I would fall to the hallway. Finally, I decided not to try the stairs again, but to find out if I had other options.

"Frightened, I walked down a corridor.

"The place was dimly lit and the farther I walked, the darker it became. At the end of the hall, I found three arched doorways. They each had moss growing around the edges of the doors and the lanterns in the hallways were extinguished. I chose a door and entered the room. There was just enough light to make out that the room was shaped like a hexagon with six walls, and that opposite me, there was another open door. But the room beyond that doorway was pitch black and scary.

"I walked into the room and lost my balance, falling onto the floor again. I began to stand, but froze when I discovered two feet away, the eyes of a wolf-like creature, a creature that was growling at me. I noticed a thin wire mesh dividing me from the wolf.

"Then I woke up," I said, at the breakfast table. "What could it mean?"

My father considered the dream for a moment, and then said, "This dream was a warning. It's a premonition of times to come."

"Really?"

"We all dream, but sometimes we have spiritual dreams with messages about our future," he said. "In my opinion, these are the best dreams to have because they present us with a lesson to learn. What lesson the dream is presenting, you'll have to figure out. But this dream sounds like it has to do with a teacher in your life. This teacher is someone you want to follow, but you're having difficulty doing it. After you fail, you're presented with other options. But you have difficulty going in the direction you want to go. That's why you slipped and fell several times. The dream is trying to prepare you for a future lesson."

"That's a very interesting interpretation." I nodded, taking his words seriously. He could have also said that because I desperately needed someone to see and hear my pain, I began to fall into a place of sadness. He wouldn't know. My father was also isolating himself in his bedroom and kept the door closed. Later, I would discover this style of neglect stunted a child's growth and caused them to feel more social anxiety and prone to depression. My depression became apparent around the time I began living with my father. I slept a lot.

I have found that as we grow older, we find ways to mask our insecurities. These masks can sometimes be layered with addictions, false personas, and personality quirks. Sometimes, we just go blank, and for a time, I was going blank. I would turn into a statue. When my father yelled, I would remain frozen. Mute. At times, living with my father, I felt like I was in the Hell world in which that monk was trapped. The only thing was, I wasn't dead yet.

I often wondered, when I died, would I end up going to that Hell?

I tried not to feel the sting of my father's words when he yelled, but he used intimidation like a bulldozer. I could tell that he saw himself as the kind of guy who got things done. It didn't matter to him that he'd have to run over a few poor fools in the process. If other people didn't know how to follow along or get out of the way, that was their problem. I was just the road kill left in his wake. I didn't know how to get out of the way or follow along. And because we lived together, I got flattened every time he drove that bulldozer through the house.

My inner turmoil didn't help my confidence. I began to read more, to transport myself into trying to understand this mystery of life after death. I was no longer just a kid growing up in Miami, I was a soul on a journey. I made a silent vow to myself. I would unravel the mysteries of the afterlife, no matter how scary or challenging the path might be. But would I be opening Pandora's box? The more I learned the more questions I had, and the more uncertain everything else became. The solid ground of reality that I had believed in was shifting beneath my feet and the rocky waters at home wasn't helping.

CHAPTER III

LSD AT DISNEYLAND

Over the next three years, my life completely changed. I no longer lived in Florida. I moved at age 15 with my father to Agoura Hills, California. We were tucked away in an apartment on the corner of Thousand Oaks Boulevard and Kanan Road. My dad had painted an ocean mural on one of the walls in my room that reminded me of happier times in Miami. Over the hills lay Los Angeles and Hollywood, just waiting for the right young actor to come along my dad kept telling me.

But my self-esteem issues and my obsessions about the afterlife were still with me in this new land, but for the moment, they were on hold because I found something new to explore: drugs.

It was 1991. The last decade of the last century had begun, but if you were to see me in high school, you might have thought it was 1969. In the Valley, I had discovered remnants of that earlier time—the complicated era of hippies promoting peace and love, not war. The counter-culture side of the wider baby boomer generation had attempted to start a movement of expanded consciousness and free love, among other ideals. They left in their wake a bunch of cool books, epic music, and drug-using parents who thought they were cool. They gave birth to Generation X. That's me, at 16; I was a by-product of that "consciousness movement," newly transplanted in liberal California.

In high school, I wanted to have a good time and make new friends, so I hung around with the druggy kids. I had shoulder length hair and a green Volkswagen bug that I would hot box after school. For anyone unfamiliar with the term, this meant I would sit in my forest green bug I had purchased with my acting money and smoked marijuana with my friends, rolling up the windows to intensify the effect of the smoke.

At the end of my sophomore year in high school, I had the great idea to go to Disneyland and drop acid. My small group of friends— more like my band of hooligans—sat in my car in the parking lot of the Happiest Place on Earth and we put LSD tabs with a little bomb drawn on each one onto our tongues and swallowed them. We chugged a quart of Minute Maid orange juice, got our gear, and walked toward the park's main entrance.

This wasn't the first time I had taken acid, but it would be my last. I was about to enter a world I hadn't known was possible, like Alice about to fall into the rabbit hole. How deep I would fall, I didn't know. Whatever was going to happen, though, it was too late to stop it. The bomb had been dropped. Me and my teenager friends didn't have a clue that we might not be able to handle it, that we didn't have a strong enough sense of self to cope with the extreme distortion of reality that can happen on a synthetic drug, especially in a public setting like Disney Land.

The main entrance gates were just ahead and my friends walked to the ticket counter. I peeled away from the group and walked past the ticket takers to the last turnstile, which was unoccupied. I sat there and waited.

Was I waiting for my friends?

That's certainly what it looked like to the Disney workers. I placed my feet up on the turn style and waited some more. The line was long in front of me, and the man taking tickets had his back to me, preoccupied, so he didn't notice when I moved my feet to the other side of the turnstile, dropped down, and casually walked into the park without a ticket.

My friends joined me, impressed that I'd managed to sneak into the park. I shrugged it off as we walked onto Main Street like four rebels without a clue. We had done it, but none of my friends knew what we were actually doing, and neither did I. While I led the way, Chris grinned at Ryan, who then punched Alberto in the shoulder.

The day passed in a kind of dreamy haze.

Hours later, in a restroom, I threw up the Minute Maid, and to me it looked like an unnatural orange sludge that had congealed with the LSD in my stomach. I realized we hadn't eaten. Ryan and Alberto busied themselves with a map, trying to figure out where to go next. I'd never actually hung out with either of them before. We met at school. And I had only known Chris for less than a year. In a long line for one of the rides, Ryan and I couldn't stop laughing. We weren't talking, just laughing. Cramped in the line with adults on all sides, Chris grew increasingly self-conscious about our behavior. We were all high on acid — what did he expect?!

A bad acid trip is not all that uncommon, but because we were so young, none of us knew how to deal with it. When the sun began to set, we were still high and still no one was talking much.

At one point, I thought I had shark teeth in my mouth.

I decided to find a restroom and pack a pipe I made with water faucet parts from Home Depot. Of course, this was well before weed was legal. Smoking pot in public wasn't necessarily a good idea, yet, right after sunset, as we walked down one of the large paths to another land, I pulled out the pipe and lighter and took a hit. When I looked up, my eyes locked with a little boy and he seemed to be terrified of me. His dad also stared — perhaps scared for his little boy — as if I were a monster or something, and the guilt felt visceral like my head was a spinning top scattering any iota of integrity.

I exhaled without thinking and the smoke blew directly into the dad's face. His jaw went tight. I stared at him, blankly. I was sure he wanted to punch me in the face. I glanced down at the boy again, and I realized, in that moment, that I was fucked.

I passed the pipe to my friends.

I couldn't feel my body. When I looked out into the park, everything had light tracers, and the lights themselves were super bright. That kid's face embedded itself in my mind: Helpless little eyes staring up at me as if I were a villain. I couldn't stop thinking about the kid no matter how hard I tried. I was convinced I had corrupted that boy's innocence. I was the bad guy in his childhood dreams, the monstrosity he feared at night.

As the marijuana took effect, guilt settled in like sludge in a swamp, and so did a peculiar feeling of paranoia. My eyes were popping. We boarded a Skyway — a ride that wouldn't exist in a couple of years — and we quickly disappeared into the trees. I breathed a sigh of relief to be away from the crowd, but that relieve was short lived as the LSD intensified it's grip on my senses.

The world around me began to warp and twist. The trees we passed seemed to be breathing, their branches became arms reaching out to strangle me. Colors bled into one another like a warm torn corpse, creating melting swirling patterns. Screams of joy became wails of anguish.

I wasn't paranoid about getting in trouble with the cops; instead, I was convinced I had just entered the purgatory of the damned, like the one that belonged to that monk. It felt as if I had stepped out of the real world and into another depraved darker dimension filled with the misery of the infernal regions, a nightmarish symphony of tearing flesh. I checked to see if I was still physically alive, yes I was in the real world, obviously, but mentally the swamps of Hades sucked me up and consumed me in sludge like a toad. I was submerged in this fowl place of torment with no way out. Time itself seemed to stretch and slow with the agony of this afflicted condition. But I remained silent like a mute gimp and said nothing to my friends about the ruinous limbo that my mind had transported and collapsed into. The safety bar of the Skyway felt frozen but also burning hot against my palms as I gripped it. I wanted off this amusement park called life. The faces of my friends began to melt and reform, their features twisting into grotesque masks that leered at me in the shadows. I squeezed my eyes shut, but the visions in the back of my eyelids were worse than reality, which at least held a faint resemblance to something familiar and solid.

At 16, I hadn't formed a strong sense of self-esteem yet, and on acid, my subconscious mind was open: I felt as if I were being re-programmed. What happened after we stepped off the Skyway might not have happened if I were a little bit older, but... I began to feel like a total loser.

I hated myself to the core. What had I become? The brutality and onslaught of negative thinking was relentless. This wasn't why I had come to Disneyland. I just wanted to have fun. What had I done? What was I doing? I didn't know, for sure.

I had become one of the bad kids at the Pinocchio theme park, and just like them, I was about to be turned into a freakish donkey. I began to transform. My teeth no longer felt human, but were shark's teeth. I ran my tongue along my teeth back and forth for fifteen minutes convinced of this traumatic transformation going on within my psyche. Mentally I could feel myself changing, becoming an aberration of what I dreaded most, the most terrifying, most unspeakably hideous freak show of them all.

All my reading for the last three years told me that I was walking with my friends down a path that sunk down into the lower realms. I was going there. No question. I had nothing but self-loathing and fear whirl pooling in my head, which began to rot my confidence to its core. I hunkered down, trembling, then lurching, in place, feeling trapped by a particular unsettling mood of darkness that created such extreme fear that all I wanted to do was scream as loud as I could and run away! But I couldn't make myself scream in a crowded line at Disneyland, and there was nowhere to run.

My friends were deathly quiet as I was spiraling down into the pit of my newly dug psychic burial chamber. The mixture of drugs had taken hold of their minds too and I could see their eyes twitch around like insects had eaten out their brains. But inside me was a death note curse like some never-ending mantra that repeated itself in my brain, in perpetuity, like an acid rain of suffering and evil torture, dissolving my soul until that last flickering spark got blown out. What had been there was completely washed away into the gutters, and it was just gone. Park rides, the cartoon characters, the happy trail smiles, the evil clown laughing and the castle of ghosts started spinning around my head in a nightmare, mocking my demise.

It was all over. Who I was, the self I had known was gone and deceased into the fairytale land necropolis. Disneyland became the coldest, darkest burial ground where the grim reaper could be found laughing in delight, the place where people go to pretend that their reality at home isn't a dream. I can't puke out to you enough words to describe what exactly I was tormented by, and, even if I could, you wouldn't want to know. And if you did know that what I was feeling was not a feeling but a state of being, you'd beg me to stop.

The next morning, when I opened my eyes I felt different. Somehow, I was not the same. Who I thought I was yesterday had vanished and who I was now I didn't recognize. A sense of anticipation hung heavy, as I gazed into the mirror in my bathroom. I saw a disturbed and unfamiliar reflection staring back at me. The person I had been was a mere shell, a collection of idle pointless thoughts, innocent beliefs, and limited experiences that no longer resonated with this darker reality that had settled inside my skin. With each passing moment, I could not ignore the call that echoed constantly, beckoning me to embrace that darkness and continue to feel the torment I had felt at Disney Land the previous evening. Tortured cries filled my mind silently, as a chorus of anguish arose in response to this ghastly realization. As the minutes stretched into an eternity, the emotional torment intensified and had settled in to find its new home.

I believe I had fallen into what is clinically called an inferiority complex or a social anxiety disorder. It felt as if I would never be content in my own skin again. It felt permanent. I was so insecure and afraid that other people didn't like me that I embraced the idea of becoming a loner.

Later, not knowing what else to do, I told my father everything. At first, he was supportive, even sympathetic, but after a week or two, he became increasingly paranoid about my drug use and he tapped the house landline. I know this because I found the recorder. I confronted my dad and he said he would turn off the recorder and put it away. It didn't help that several months earlier, my father and I took a road trip and visited his old meditation friends. That night, I went off with his friends two sons who were my childhood friends. Later, he discovered I had given them LSD. He denied it at first. He thought that my childhood friends must have supplied the LSD, believing I was still an innocent 16 year old. But then I had to admit the truth.

Several months later, I found an extra phone line not connected to the wall. It was white and didn't look like the other cords. Reaching behind the desk, I followed the cord with my fingers down into the rug. I pulled the desk back and ripped it out from under the carpet. I followed the cord along the wall and into the hallway and all the way into my dad's bedroom. He must have felt like he was being clever. There, I discovered the cord went into the back of his underwear drawer where he hid the recording device. I had heard of other parents who didn't know what to do to help their children, and that some of them turned their kids into the police. My father was attempting to find out who had given me the drugs. He didn't know I had purchased an entire sheet of acid at school myself, and I had taken the few tabs that were left to party with my friends at Disneyland.

One day, my father simply snapped and demanded to know the names of my friends I'd gone with and what was the name of the kid who sold me the LSD. I refused to tell him because these were my friends. His anger grew. He screamed.

Scared, I looked down at the ground under the pressure. At that moment, Chris Edgar, one of the kids who I'd gone to Disneyland with called me. My father answered the phone and then, instead of hanging up, placed the phone on the counter.

Chris was listening.

My father laid into me, furiously demanding to know my friends' names. I cracked and told him their first names never having seen this sort of rage before, but I refused to give him their last names. That was all Chris needed to hear on the other end of the phone. He immediately called the other kids and told them to hide their drugs. My father didn't actually do anything, but he had set the phone down off the hook on purpose, allowing Chris to hear him yell at me. Mission accomplished.

At high school, rumors spread that I had snitched out my friends who sold drugs. I saw it as a blessing in disguise because after that bad acid trip, I wanted to quit completely. In order to do that, I had to stop hanging out with the stoners. In that sense, it worked out. No one was arrested, and I was now a loner with no friends.

A few months later, a kid named David Bloomfield was arrested for selling weed at school. He had nothing to do with the acid I bought or my trip to Disneyland. He was just a friend of Chris Edgar. I had only smoked weed with David a few times. Because of Chris's rumor that I was a rat, he got it into his head I was the one who got him arrested. Maybe that's what Chris Edgar told him. Luckily, one of the kids I used to hang out with warned me that David's older brother and a gang of Malibu surfers were going to jump me. I kept my eye out, but didn't see them all day... at least not until my last class.

Five guys I didn't recognize surrounded me.

We were alone and no one was going to stop them from kicking my ass. I had to act fast. I knew I was innocent, but what could I do?

One of the biggest guys turned to his friend and said, "Is this the guy?"

Before the friend could answer, I shouted, "You guys don't know what the hell you're talking about. I didn't do shit! I didn't rat anyone out. It's all some mother-fucking rumor. I didn't even know David was selling weed. You guys got shit on me."

I walked past the biggest guy as fast as I could and into the classroom. They were so stunned by my reaction that they didn't bother me again.

At the end of the year, I was with some friends at the beach, where they said, "We don't know why we believed that rumor about you. You're cool, man."

"Don't worry about it," I said.

I still didn't hang out with them and do drugs anymore. I was a loner now.

After David got out of jail, he returned to the classroom, and noticed that I was sitting in the back row next to one of the biggest flirts in our grade. Her name was Courtney Savoy, who was had a split personality as both a new age hippie and a preppy chick. She had very large boobs. These are things you notice as a teenager. Courtney didn't notice the following exchange, but... I had a staring contest with David, the stoner. His eyes looked different to me. Guilty, somehow? Perhaps David realized it wasn't me who had gotten him arrested? Either way, his eyes seemed to be covering something up.

Was it something he didn't want to admit?

I looked away and saw a kid Courtney and I nicknamed Rocky Road, because one time he brought Rocky Road ice cream into class and shared it with us. He had a couple of spare spoons and he gave them to us and no one else, and we formed a little group. I called him Rocky, for short. He revealed to me that Courtney always made him smile. I think he secretly had a crush on Courtney.

The truth? She made me smile, too. Joy just seemed to shoot out of her like a soda that had been shaken violently and opened. I liked Courtney the previous year, too, and we almost dated, but one of the senior class football players got to her first. She was one of the biggest flirts in our grade and was always positive. I think she almost won Homecoming Queen. I almost had a shot at winning Homecoming King, but I was one of the bad boys and wasn't part of the popular crowd, so I didn't make the cut.

Courtney picked up a pencil out of her pencil case and began drawing rainbows, then she looked at Rocky and said, "I really love rainbows. I do. Do you? Because I really do."

Rocky smiled and said, "Rainbows are natural optical phenomena that occur when sunlight interacts with water droplets in the air."

"You're so smart," She said.

"Rainbows were also used on the cover of Grateful Dead's album, Dark Side of the Moon," he offered.

"You're smart and cool Mr. Rocky Road," Courtney smiled. "When are you going to bring ice cream to class again?"

"I don't know. Maybe on the last day of class?"

"Ah, that would be fun!"

My heart was still pounding, because I thought I was about to get into a fight with the recently paroled school drug dealer. I would have done it, if I had to stand up for myself, but it seemed David was content to ignore me, so I would be content to ignore him.

"You remind me of rainbows," she said to Rocky, as she drew a rainbow on a piece of paper.

"Thanks, Courtney," Rocky said, smiling from ear to ear. He looked at me like he had just won the lottery.

I laughed silently, glad to forget about David. Courtney smiled at Rocky, and then she smiled at me.

"You also remind me of rainbows, Greg," she said, beaming.

I was the only one not really smiling, because I was still trying to get my pounding heart to calm down.

"It's too bad it never rains in Agoura," I said. " We'd have rainbows every day."

After class, David walked up to me just outside the door. I braced myself for a fight. He told me he thought I was cool for not being mad at him for almost having me jumped. Apparently, the rumor had worn off, and the drug dealers forgot about me.

Another day at school, during a fifteen-minute recess, I entered the restroom in the freshman quad. For some reason, the walls were painted all black—I think it was to battle a growing graffiti problem, which was not a bad idea, since most of the kids at this predominately white school only knew how to make graffiti with a black sharpie.

A kid named Justin, who I had smoked weed with once before, was standing alone in the dark. It was weird that he was just there, doing nothing.

I nodded to him. He stared at me while I took a piss. I looked at him, blankly, and then looked away. Justin was the kind of kid who looked like he shouldn't be in high school anymore. Maybe it was all the drug use that made him look older, but he had an aura of a crack head about him. His long dirty blond hair fell over sunken dark eyes and he literally looked evil. He had bully written all over his face. He kept staring and it began to creep me out.

What the fuck was wrong with this kid?

If there was one thing I couldn't stand, it was bullies. I had once broken up with a group of friends—J.R. Owens, Larry Albitre, Arash, and me. Arash was the Hispanic class clown. Larry was the only American Indian in our school, aside from me, but I was only one-sixteenth Cherokee and looked more White than anything else. Larry was Chumash and Apache. And J.R. was the only black kid in our grade. We would have had a pretty dope group of fools. One day, during lunch, I saw Larry and Arash picking on some kid with another guy, so I stopped talking to them.

J.R. was pissed off, because our group would have been extremely popular and gotten into all the parties. But I just hated bullies.

After I relieved myself, and washed my hands in a grimy high school sink, I felt something come down around my throat from behind and tighten, instantly choking me. Confused, I pivoted to see what was happening. I threw my arms up, knocking Justin's arms backwards. It was then that I realized Justin had walked up behind me and wrapped a metal coat hanger around my neck and pulled it tight.

What the fuck was wrong with this meathead?

He laughed this sinister chuckle and looked like he was totally fucking high.

This might have happened because of the rumors being spread about me amongst the stoner clique. Or maybe it was because I looked like a nice guy who was a prime target for a bully. Either way, something inside snapped.

Normally, I was the nicest guy you would ever meet. Most people thought of me the same way people thought of my mother, like an angel. But, lurking inside, there were things I had yet to discover about myself — things hidden in the shadows. In that moment, I was shocked to find out just how much of a badass I really was.

I forgot myself for a moment, and I'm not sure exactly what I said; I only remember the rage that vibrated off of me. Some sort of explosive force emanated from the core of my chest, and I verbally assaulted him with a barrage of insults that echoed so loudly, and with such ferocity, that he almost fell backwards into a stinking, scummy toilet.

The look on Justin's face was priceless.

When I stopped my rant, I paused and marveled. I didn't know I had it in me to tell someone off like that. I slammed the restroom door open and stomped back out into the freshman quad. The sunlight was a nice reminder that I didn't want to get lost on the dark side of things. When I looked back, Justin remained in his little hole-in-the-wall rat's den.

Was he really not going to come after me? Had I scared him that badly?

I think he got kicked out of school shortly after that choking incident, because I never saw or spoke to him again. Or maybe he died and went to hell?

I didn't know and I didn't care.

In my junior year, I found new friends, the only other out-casts at the school—retro punk hipster girls who sat on a nearby hill. Some of the girls thought I was cute even though I dressed more like a grunge hippie with long hair down to my chin. We didn't know each other that well, but I started to open up to two of them. Adi and Shelly took an interest in me.

I was still depressed, though, after that bad LSD trip. The depression kept getting worse, and it came with massive mood swings that left me wanting to shrivel into a ball and hide in a dark corner and never come out. It seemed that this metaphorical rats den was a place I willingly crawled into, and crawling back out wasn't going to be as easy as I thought. And while I was down there in that swamp, I'd meet some randoms, unsavory types, who didn't have my best interests in mind.

So stayed in my room and buried myself in books I bought at *The Bodhi Tree*, a New Age bookstore on the other side of the hill.

After I read Paramahansa Yogananda's *Autobiography of a Yogi*, I became convinced that meditation directly affected which level you go to after death. It is as if the levels of life, now and after we die, are like the skin of an onion. Humans are at the center of the onion, and we must reach the outside layer, somehow moving upward, level after level.

Please forgive the mixed metaphor, but meditation is like an elevator at the center of this onion that can more rapidly transport you from the center to the outside, allowing you to quickly evolve and reach the outermost layer—the highest levels of reality.

In the afternoon, the last class of the day was in the far corner of campus. Art was my favorite class. I sat next to one of the prettiest blond girls in high school named Rachel. Rachel wasn't just pretty, but she was also very cool.

After class as I headed up the hill back to my house, I

felt a tug at the back of my shirt. The next thing I knew I was being shoved up against a chain link fence by Rachel's overzealous boyfriend. He snarled like a dog. I was wondering if he was going to punch me.

Instead, in between his spitting and ranting he threatened that if I didn't stop speaking to Rachel outside class he would "end me." Whatever that meant.

The next day in class felt a little awkward. It wasn't that I didn't want to talk to Rachel in class, I just kept thinking about her boyfriend's threat.

From time to time outside of class, she'd catch me looking at her, and smile and wave. I'd smile and wave back. I think she liked me because she said hello to me every time we saw each other. I didn't mind of course. I just wished she didn't have a boyfriend. This made my friends jealous since she was one of the hottest girls at school.

I forget Rachel's boyfriend's name, something like Steve. He apparently hated me she said. He didn't approach me again after that first incident, but it made it difficult to leave class because her boyfriend was usually waiting for her. I'd always make up some excuse to stay behind until after she had left so that I could avoid talking to her outside of the classroom. I mean because we sat next to each other we became friends and got used to talking to each other every day. It was kind of hard to avoid talking to her. I tried and failed on a daily basis.

That year I wore baggy jeans, a size too big, which meant my belt always was bunched up. To cover that up I'd wear big t-shirts. It was the style. Mike Shinoda was one of the better artists in my art class. He also became famous later for cofounding the rock band Linkin Park.

I thought he was cool so I offered him a job working with the company I worked for drawing comic book-style gangster animals on t-shirts. I later regretted my choice because Mike was a much better artist than me, and I ended up not getting any of my characters designs printed on any of the t-shirts. This is what I was thinking about when Rachel sat down next to me in art class the next day.

"Is everything alright," she asked.

"Yeah, I'm fine."

"You look upset," she set her backpack down under the seat.

"I was just thinking about something."

"You're always thinking about something. You're such a deep-thinking guy. Hey, I heard you smoked pot. I need some," she whispered.

"I don't smoke anymore. Now I just meditate," I said, finally looking at her. This is something I often found myself saying. I had become one of the popular stoners around campus and I didn't want to be stuck with this stoner image anymore.

Rachel was wearing a tight V-neck shirt, which meant I could see an ample amount of cleavage. Her long blond hair fell down passed her shoulders in cascading twirls, and her lipstick had glitter, which sparkled. Her eyes were a sky blue and when I looked into them, I felt as if I was hypnotized like some lost field mouse. She liked giving hugs in class and smashing her chest up into me, wrapping her arms around me like a python. I didn't complain. Needless to say, she looked sexy as hell. I could understand why Steve was insecure. I wasn't mad at him, but maybe a little jealous.

"Oh yeah, you meditate? What's that about?" She said casually as she pulled out her drawing pad and began to pretend to look busy doing nothing in particular.

"I just started doing it. Kind of hard to explain but I'm reading a book about it that's pretty cool, have you heard of 'The Autobiography of a Yogi'?"

"No, tell me about it."

"You'd probably think it's boring," I said and focused on the teacher who seemed to be in her own world. Art class was really a joke. Our teacher never really taught us anything. We just sat there for an hour doing nothing but doodling.

"I'm sure it's more interesting than class," Renee said.

"Well, the book describes this Yogi's life, starting with his childhood, and finding his own Guru, Swami Yukteswar."

"Yogi, like he did yoga?"

"No, he practiced meditation. In India Yoga means meditation. But American's have copied the word, giving it a new meaning based on capitalism and making money and so now Yoga just means stretching. Anyway, the book explains how this Yogi, his name was Yogananda, became a monk, and about his practice of Kriya meditation, as well as all the other crazy meditation freaks he met in India."

"Well that sounds really interesting Greg. You need to tell me all about it."

"Right now?" I turned and looked into her eyes forgetting where I was for a moment.

"Yeah," she said looking back at me with interest. "I wanna hear about it.

Then, if you promise not to tell anyone, I'll tell you about my DMT trip."

"Wait, you tried DMT?"

"Oh, don't pretend to be a saint. I know you did LSD."

"Well, yeah…" I stuttered. "Who told you about that?"

"Everybody knows you're a stoner Greg. I guess you used to be. Anyway, now tell me about this book. Sounds totally fascinating."

"Okay, okay, so this guy was a really good meditator. Even from a young age. He practiced every day. And he lived his whole life with his guru in Puri, on the east coast of India. He's super dedicated to his teacher, and then he goes to America, and when he comes back, his teacher died. I mean, like he died right when Yogananda came back. He was totally bummed that he didn't go right away to see him when he could have. Instead he went to some festival and missed his chance to see his teacher one last time, so he's feeling guilty. He was so upset about his teacher passing, he's crying every day and stuff and then one day, he is visited by his guru."

"What's a guru?"

"It just means teacher. But in India the word holds spiritual meaning."

"So if his guru died, how did he visit him?"

"Exactly! So, his guru resurrected, like he manifested in the body again. This was back in 1936, in a hotel room in Bombay. Bombay is on the other side of the country. So, it's pretty far away from the meditation center in Puri. Anyway, Yogananda is totally amazed to see his guru Sri Yukteswar appear before him in the flesh. He resurrected like Jesus. Can you believe that?"

"Whoa, that is just like Jesus," she said. Rachel had given up on the idea of pretending to look busy. She was far too interested in my story now.

"That's right. Pretty wild. Jesus isn't the only one who can resurrect. So after Yogananda hugs his teacher and apologizes for not coming back to see him right away, he begins questioning his guru about what happens after we die. This subject is really interesting for me. I'm obsessed with figuring out what happens after we die. I mean nobody really knows what's going to happen, right?"

"I know. It's weird to think about that," Rachel agreed.

"Yeah, so check this out, that's when his guru describes that the different dimensions are divided into three levels — the three-dimensional physical world, the four-dimensional spirit world called the astral plane, and the fifth-dimensional spiritual world of the causal plane — and these levels eventually lead to a place where you can live eternally and blissfully as a part of God-consciousness in the higher celestial realms."

"That's crazy Greg. I like it, more, more," she leaned over and nudged her chest into my arm, encouraging me to continue. Was she flirting with me?

"Sri Yukteswar told Yogananda that to emerge from these three dimensions, a person must have countless earthly, astral and causal incarnations. A spiritual Master who is free of such bondage may return to Earth as a prophet in order to help other humans return to God. Like Sri Yukteswar, a Master might choose to reside in the astral cosmos, help clean off the burdens the astral inhabitant's karma, and help them move on to the celestial causal spheres beyond. A freed soul may also return to the causal plane to help the beings there move upward toward absolute freedom.

"Yogananda's guru said that he was now a guide for souls who have come down from the causal dimension to reincarnate in the astral plane, as opposed to humans who have just died on Earth and who rise to the astral plane."

"That's confusing," Rachel commented. "So, there are multiple spiritual dimensions that our spirit can fly up to and fall out of?

"Apparently, and most human beings after death don't learn to appreciate the astral world, or suffer there, and so they keep coming back to Earth. They reincarnate repeatedly until they've learned their lessons and become pure enough to progress higher. In the same way, souls return to the astral world after falling down from the causal. They take on a new astral body to pay their dues."

"My brain hurts just listening to you," Rachel commented.

"Do you want me to stop," I asked.

"No, I just feel like I'm cramming for an exam in Spirituality 101."

I laughed. "So astral spirits can't really appreciate or focus on the quality of spiritual joy in the causal plane. They can't let go of their astral memories and attachment to the astral paradise. Only when there is no more desire for astral experience, and no karma to pay there, can a soul stay in the causal world. Sri Yukteswar explained all this to Yogananda, that he was helping the astrally re-incarnated souls lose their astral body to regain the causal plane where they would have the opportunity to once and for all rid themselves of the causal body and merge with the eternal.

"Then Yogananda tells his Guru how sad he is. Yukteswar reminds Yogananda that we are dreaming on Earth, that he only saw a dream-body die, and that he resurrected himself in a new body on a finer dream-planet of God in another realm called Hiranyaloka or the illumined astral planet. He urged Yogananda to differentiate... between dreams and Reality, not to grieve for him, and to share the news of his resurrection. He declares that this will provide new hope for the death-fearing dreamers of the world. What dreams may come," I winked, quoting Hamlet.

"I am enthralled by your mind," Rachel gushed. "I also have a brain ache. But keep going."

"So Yogananda agrees to write a book. Yukteswar spent two hours with him in that hotel room in Bombay. Yukteswar then says he's leaving and disappears while Yogananda hugs him. The Master's voice lingers, telling his former student to call upon him when he reaches 'Samadhi,' a state when ego disappears and only consciousness remains, and the Master will appear to him. He asks Yogananda to tell everyone that, whoever can enter Samadhi, may come to the finer dream-created planet of Hiranyaloka and find him. The end. That's it."

"Whoa, how did you remember that entire story?" Rachel said in astonishment. "That was amazing Greg!"

"I'm really interested in this life after death stuff. It's an obsession of mine I guess. I've discovered that there are levels after you die. And I want to find the key that will unlock these higher spiritual worlds. I think this story holds that key."

CHAPTER IV

RESURRECTION

The words of Sri Yukteswar captivated me as a teenager. I told my father I wanted to learn how to meditate after reading that story, and I asked him to introduce me to his Guru, Prem Pal Singh Rawat. It's probably safe to say that most parents of teenagers in Agoura Hills didn't have a Guru, but fate had it that my father did. In fact, Prem Rawat was formerly known as Maharaji. He was one of the most famous Gurus in the United States back in the 1970s.

And my father was so devoted to this Guru that the man was of paramount importance in his life. In fact, my dad worked at the Guru's house for 15 years as a security guard. When we moved to California, my father always made sure he was on time for work. He often told me he was generally well liked by the community.

During one of L.A.'s great fires, a burn which began in Thousand Oaks and moved all the way to Malibu, he purposely drove over Kanan Road into the fires, passing police barricades in order to go to his Guru's house in Malibu. He and two other security guards, who were both disciples of Prem Rawat, risked their lives to protect that house. Putting your life on the line to protect your Guru was considered an act of ultimate devotion. However, less than a month later, along with several other men, my father was fired. The Rawat household had decided to bring in a professional team of security guards. It was a business decision.

After reading *Autobiography of a Yogi*, I was beginning to fit together pieces of the puzzle I'd been trying to solve ever since I had heard about my mother's out of the body experiences. At last I had some good answers to my questions about what happens after death. I began a quest for a competent living master, one capable of preparing me for the beyond through meditation, and finally to higher spiritual realms after leaving the body behind for good.

How would I find such a person? I wasn't sure, but I knew where to start.

I asked my father to take me to the weekly gatherings he attended, where followers played a video of Prem Rawat. Since everyone there was my father's age, I didn't socialize with anyone at the meetings. I just watched the videos intently. I was amused to see Nick Nolte show up once.

My father became my first spiritual teacher. One night he asked me to sit down in his room, dimly lit by a shaded lamp. I was afraid my dad meant to lecture or scold me, but when I walked in the space I felt calm and peaceful. I didn't say anything. I just sat quietly and listened.

"If you want to learn how to meditate," he said, "there is a simple meditation where you count your breaths. Try not to think about anything but the breath. If you have a thought, start over from the number one. The goal is to count to 10 without thinking anything."

Because he had just been meditating, the room felt charged with good energy. He began to lecture on the higher consciousness. I generally caught on and felt inspired. Like my mother and her stories about out-of-body experiences, my father and I now had something very cool in common. It seemed to me like my father was an experienced and skillful meditator. Truthfully, I didn't know exactly what meditation was or what he was talking about most of the time. I tried to follow the logic, but I picked up more from my father's state of being than anything else. His chill, hyper low key vibe made me feel very comfortable. This super silent energy contrasted with his emotional abusive side, but seeing that contrast actually helped me pick up on just how relaxed his essential spiritual vibe really was.

I didn't realize I had such a practical spiritual father up until this point, and I felt lucky for that. He didn't have complex beliefs and didn't force me to go to church. When he was meditating, though, I could feel the beautiful vibrations emanating from his room. It felt like he was some sort of Zen Master on one level and totally different on another.

I wasn't quite sure how I was able to feel such things. I couldn't even describe what it was I was feeling. Somehow, it was quietly beautiful. Even though there was this underlying tension between us because of all the other drama, for now at least I was able to relax around him and absorb this positive flow. These, I think, were some of our happiest moments together.

"Could you explain what you do when you meditate?" I asked.

"Well, the first thing you have to understand is that it's important to me," he said. "If it's important to you, then you do it. It's like going to work. If you have to be at work at eight o'clock, you don't think about going to work. You go every day because you know the paycheck is important."

"Good point," I said, nodding.

"You make it a habit because you've already decided that it's important. Otherwise, you're going to be homeless and hungry."

"Right, but once you sit down, what's the focus?" I asked. "How do you get your mind so quiet?"

"It's practice," he said. "Like anything else. Because your brain deals with so many different things, you have to boil down what you're doing to the most common actions. And those are the things you focus on, and you keep those things the same every time. You have a powerful unconscious mind. If you don't train that mind, you become your own worst enemy. But, if you train yourself, then you will have a friend who will help you. So, if you practice every day, then you learn a little bit more every day."

"So daily practice is important," I repeated.

"When you push the up button on an elevator, you don't have to think, 'I want to go up.' The elevator will do it automatically. In real meditation, when you sit down and practice the method, you get uplifted. It becomes automatic. You don't have to think about it."

"What if I don't practice the method properly?"

"No effort is wrong, because you're going in the right direction. In one sense, it's an impossible task for your mind to conceive. People want to define what meditation is, but you can't do that. You can't conceive it, because where you're going is into the realm of the inconceivable."

"Right," I agreed, but I had a confused look on my face.

"I'm going to conceive of the inconceivable," my father said. "That's what most people are thinking. No, you can't do that. You have to have an open mind. Accept the fact that your brain isn't going to understand it. And that's okay. It's like when people discuss God. They have different concepts of God... so, how do you know one concept is right and another concept is wrong? Do you know?"

I shrugged. "I don't know."

"God is inconceivable. Every concept is wrong."

We both laughed.

"You can't conceive it," he continued. "You can only experience it. And once you've experienced it, then your mind will feel satisfied. And, after a few days, you'll forget about that also and that memory becomes just a concept."

"Whoa, that's confusing," I said. "So, your memory isn't even real?"

"It's not," he agreed. "But you're thinking, 'Oh, I have this memory of God so I understand.' No, the memory should inspire you to have that experience again. The joy is in the experience, I want to have that today. I don't want to have just a memory of that. That joy increases the more I practice. And the more I practice, the easier it becomes and the more beautiful it becomes."

This gave me a new idea: "Do you think meditation will help me deal with my depression?"

"Yeah," my father said. "We think that feeling is who we are and that feeling will last forever. The key is not to identify with the feeling. It's just like when you see a movie. You feel something while you're watching the film, but when you walk out of the movie theater the emotions pass because it wasn't us. So, if we don't identify with depression, it's easier to let go of."

He continued, "Regular practice is crucial. Meditation doesn't make suffering disappear, but it lessens its impact. When you focus your mind during meditation, you're training yourself to not get caught up in negative thoughts. Over time you learn to observe your feelings without being overwhelmed by them. It's not like the suffering goes away, but it affects us less. When you focus, it takes you deeper into that experience of peace."

"So, focusing is one of the key elements in making meditation work?"

"Kind of. I'm not doing anything. I am just becoming still. It's that power that affects you, that lifts you up and takes you higher. But going higher is just a concept. You're not actually going higher. That's just a metaphorical way to talk about it."

"When you say the power... Is that related to the technique of meditation?"

"The technique is just one of the key elements you need to focus on so that you can let go of the chatter in your head and just be. Through repeated practice, you tune into that power more easily. You're not going to sit down and understand how to do it all at once. And you can't go the way I went. You have to learn your own way."

"Okay, thanks," I said. I swallowed and stood up. "I think I got it."

As I looked down at him in his chair, I saw my father in a new light. Our relationship was maturing in a way I didn't expect.

After these conversations with my father, I felt a new-found respect for him and a growing curiosity about meditation. However, I soon realized that it would be a long process before I ever learned his style of meditation because his teacher, Prem Rawat, didn't teach regularly, and the gatherings I attended left me wanting more.

I needed something more structured, so I looked around town for other meditation groups, hoping to find a place where I could actually sit down and meditate in a class.

As I continued my search, I couldn't shake the feeling that I was on the verge of discovering something transformative. I was about to open doorways to experiences I could have never imagined.

Reading in the Autobiography of a Yogi heavily influenced me, that Sri Yukteshwar's resurrection, like Jesus', powerfully demonstrated the continuity of life after death. This modern miracle offers fresh evidence of what spiritual practices directly affect our spiritual growth. By recognizing Sri Yukteshwar's miraculous resurrection as equally significant, we embrace a broader more open view of what's possible, honoring diverse paths of enlightenment.

CHAPTER V

DMT

Back at school, the moment Rachel walked into art class I felt something. I became super alert, but I didn't know why. Then she looked at me in a peculiar way, and sat down without smiling or hugging me like she normally did. Instead, she kept peeking at me as if she had something important to tell me. We quietly sat, lapsing in laziness while the teacher explained the day's lesson plan. After about six minutes we got busy doodling.

"What's up?" I asked, giving Rachel a sidelong glance. She was sullen.

"Me and that asshole, what's his face, Steven, broke up," She said with a fake smirk, lifting her head slightly so I could see the faint expression on her face. It was the kind of smirk that pretended to show disappointment but was secretly coded. Was Rachel trying to tell me… wait.

Was she flirting with me? I was confused.

"That sucks, so should I buy you dinner to cheer you up?" I teased. The words came out of my face faster than I could think them.

"You should," she smirked again, but this time she meant it. My heart pounded.

"Wanna hear my DMT story?" She bit her lip and looked at me like she'd never looked at me before. What was happening to my body? What was this rush of electricity? Part of me wanted to run, and another part wanted to grab her.

I nodded, in utter shock because Rachel had just agreed to go on a date with me and because she agreed faster than I could have ever imagined. This meant she really liked me! She began speaking in earnest to me, explaining how her ex-boyfriend took her to Harbin Hot Springs up north over the weekend. She had convinced her parents to let her go out of town on the date with her boyfriend, I guess because he would be leaving for college or something like that. But I think she told them she was just going with some friends. It actually turned out to be their final goodbye escapade.

She didn't realize she'd have to go topless at the hot spring. Her boyfriend actually forced her to jump back and forth between the hot and cold pool nine times! She did it even though she knew his ulterior motive was to make her give everyone a show of her topless assets. But she was rewarded somehow, pleasantly surprised to have had a meditative experience afterwards. If it wasn't for me explaining meditation to her, she might not have known what that was. I found it interesting that she achieved that state through the ultimate relaxation and shock of going back and forth between hot and cold springs. Then she did DMT and she felt like she became one with nature, talking to fairy spirits in the woods and seeing little purple people and flying into space like my mother had done. All of this led to her breaking up with the boyfriend.

As Rachel described her experience, I felt a mixture of fascination and envy. The way she talked about becoming one with nature, conversing with fairy spirits, and seeing purple beings resonated deeply with my own spiritual curiosity. It was as if she had stumbled upon a shortcut to the mystical realms and I'd been reading about it for years.

"That's incredible Rach," I said, leaning in closer. "Did it feel real? Like, more real than this life?"

Rachel nodded emphatically. "It was beyond real. It was like… everything I thought I knew about reality just died and shattered."

Her words sent a shiver down my spine.

"Do you think it changed you?" I asked. Wasn't this exactly what I'd been searching for? A glimpse behind the veil of ordinary existence? I thought about the monk's journey in the afterlife and my own fledgling attempts at going within. Rachel experienced in minutes what I'd been trying to understand for years. But if Rachel could access these otherworldly realms through DMT, surely I could reach them through meditation and spiritual practice.

In art class one day, I pulled out a black cat firework. Someone had given it to me earlier. I can't explain why I did it, I just did it without really thinking.

"Watch this," I said. Holding onto the wick, I thought the fire would stop at the wick and the firework wouldn't go off. It wasn't the best line of thinking.

"What are you doing?" One of the kids next to me asked.

"What does it look like," I smirked.

"Greg, you're going to do that in class?" Mike Shinoda said.

"Let's see if I hold the wick if it will still go off or will it stop."

"You're crazy Greg," Rachel rolled her eyes. But she crowded around as well. "It's still going to go off," said somebody else.

I pulled out the lighter and set the wick ablaze. It sparkled and fizzed down fast. I imagined the wick would fizzle out once it hit my fingers but I felt it burning through. I realized I had to act fast because the black cat was about to blow up in my hand so I threw it up, just above my hand and it went off with a loud bang and a puff of smoke. Everyone scattered back to their seat. I could feel the sting on my hand. The teacher let it go! Instead of going to the principal's office, after class I walked outside with Rachel.

"Greg, what were you thinking today? You trying to get kicked out of school."

"I guess you're right. I don't know. Sorry. Listen, I need your number if I'm going to take you out this weekend."

Rachel handed me her number. She had it written down, ready to give to me.

She winked and walked away. I stood there stunned. I would be taking out one of the hottest girls in school. I'm sure Courtney would be jealous. Although Courtney and I also went out on a date, she left me for an upper classman on the football team who had also went away to college.

I picked Rachel up in West Lake and took her to see a movie called, 'Sex Lies and Videotape'. Was I being too suggestive by taking her out to see that film, on a first date? I imagined we'd kiss in the movie theater but we didn't. We walked around the shopping center in Westlake village for an hour or so and I bought her ice cream. We sat by the fountain as Rachel told me a few more stories of her ex-boyfriend. I didn't say much. After the date we walked out to my car. I had specifically parked far away from everyone else so that when we got back to my car we could make out, which we did.

During our entanglement, I managed to get her bra off. I pushed her shirt up and drooled. I'd never seen a more perfect pair of breasts. I kissed them for a few minutes.

"You want to come over," I asked.

"Maybe next time," she quickly put her bra back on. My god they were perfect.

As we drove in the car back to her parents she explained that she was actually still a virgin. I was too but I didn't want to admit it. It was hard for me to believe. She had a boyfriend for almost a year and they never had sex? She also told me how she lied to her parents about the date just like she had lied about going to Harbin Hot Springs with her boyfriend, so when we got to her place I parked several blocks away. She was supposed to be out with her friend, Shama.

I dropped her off before eleven thirty, which was her cut off time before she got in trouble. She kissed me on the cheek, and made promises she'd never keep. I wanted to say things I knew I shouldn't say. I had a feeling this would be our one and only date. I wasn't wrong.

"I had fun," was the last thing she said to me.

"Cool," was all I said.

CHAPTER VI

WORMHOLES

My search led me to a Soto Zen center in Northridge with real Zen monks who had come from Japan. I would sit on a meditation mat until my legs were numb, for about forty minutes, then we'd walk in circles. That's about all we did. But we only did it on the weekends when I had time off school. I didn't go every weekend either.

Then I went to another Buddhist temple, from a Taiwan tradition, called the Hsi Lai Temple. It was quite an impressive sight to behold. Everywhere stood towering buildings with old-style Chinese roofs and dragons and gods and Buddha statues. It took me ten minutes just to walk from the parking lot to the back of the property. It was so large they even had a map of the layout.

After stopping inside the temple, I found out about their meditation classes on Sunday and joined. Mainly, we'd sit and do walking meditation. It was exactly the same thing as the other place, but they didn't have any cool books or instruction manuals. Hsi Lai just had impressive Chinese style buildings and a free buffet and the monks wore different color robes.

I'll admit, I liked the buffet because I was vegetarian and it was hard to find good vegetarian food. After I ate, I walked around the temple grounds. A female monk in brown robes stopped and talked to me. Eventually, I asked her, "How do you reach enlightenment?"

"It can take life times," she laughed. Her shaved head reflected the sunlight the way a car hood shines after a wax.

Back at the Soto Zen Center, actually called The Beginner's Mind Zen Center, I discovered the book that moved me most: *Zen Mind, Beginner's Mind*. When I read it, I loved it like an addict loves cocaine.

It was good, I mean, it was really good for me. I got it. I liked this whole idea of always having a beginner's mind, and finding enlightenment before you could find enlightenment.

The Zen Center was also not far from where I lived. The two monks who ran the place were Peter and Jane Schneider. I liked their temple. Although it was smaller than the Hsi Lai Temple, we essentially did the same thing that they did at Hsi Lai—meditating and walking. The only real difference for me was the amazing book. Shunryu Suzuki, the monk who wrote the book, knew what he was talking about. His words made sense in a profound esoteric way. I knew that all Buddhists believed in having such things as Right View, Right Conduct, Right Practice, Right Understanding, and Right Livelihood, but how one looks at these things seemed a bit tricky.

While the monk I met at the Hsi Lai Temple was like any monk I might have met at any other temple. I thought Suzuki demonstrated the correct way to see things as they are and expressed a profound understanding of Zen. His perspective took meditation to a whole new level. Because of these teachings, I realized I needed to change how I approached meditation: I'd been thinking about it all wrong.

Meditation was just a word, a vague idea. But the practice was the path to real understanding.

Like the monk at Hsi Lai suggested, the idea of enlightenment was mixed up in my head, like a complicated jigsaw puzzle that would take me many life times to figure out. But what if I could attain instant Enlightenment? Like right now. In the book, Suzuki describes his ideas regarding *Zazen*, which literally means *seated meditation*, a method used by monks to gain insight into the nature of existence.

"Just see things as they are without any effort," Suzuki wrote. "You cannot practice true Zazen, because you practice it. When you do it, you create some concrete idea of 'you' or 'I,' and you create some particular idea of practice of Zazen. So, whatever you do, or even though you do not do anything, enlightenment is there, always. This is Bodhidharma's understanding of enlightenment."

I was deeply moved by these words. I knew they would lead me toward the right path. Even though I looked for an Indian Guru every time I went to the spiritual bookstore near my house, in this book written by a Japanese monk, I felt I had something concrete to start my journey, as if I had been given a magic key.

I picked up a few more books on Buddhism, like, *If You Meet the Buddha on the Road, Kill Him*, written by psychotherapist Sheldon B. Kopp. That was a crazy book, and it introduced me to the idea of Crazy Zen.

Crazy Zen monks didn't follow Right Conduct and didn't have Right Understanding. They took this notion that everything is Zazen to mean that you could do anything. You can sin, eat, drink, smoke, and join the party, because everything in life is life. If you were truly enlightened, you could do it all. There is nothing to learn and nothing anyone can teach you.

This appealed to my teenage mind a great deal.

The only problem with this path was that once you walked into a fire, you got burned. But getting burned was also part of it. You had to have complete acceptance. There were no hidden meanings or secrets. If you could accept everything—the pain and pleasure with a neutral state of mind—then you'd found the meaning of Zen. This total surrender toward your existence was what brought about an awakening. You could go work your job, go to school, make love, drink, have fun, all of it—because no understanding beyond what you already knew was really real. We were all Buddha; we just had to open our eyes to what was and accept reality.

After playing around with that ideology, I found it seemed too easy. I was looking for something more structured. I needed discipline. I had a specific understanding of things I had developed myself and needed to follow that understanding toward some, as of yet, unknown destination.

During this time, I lived two lives—a life of meditation at home and temples, and the life of an ordinary depressed teenager at school. When I was sixteen, I got initiated by Prem Rawat, who was also called, Maharaji, in an Oxnard hotel meeting room with fifteen other people. He went over the techniques and we all meditated together.

In my sophomore year at Agoura High, it felt as if my life and friends were all disappearing. The only thing that gave me hope was meditation. After learning how to meditate from my father's guru Maharaji, I would sit and meditate in my room whenever I found the time.

One evening, I wrapped a thin, white blanket around my legs and flicked off all the lights. It's an odd thing to do—to turn your lights off long before you plan to go to sleep. But tonight, I craved that isolation. I thought about this as I walked over to my meditation pillow and sat down. The room was illuminated from the light slicing downwards through the window shades, creating that cool shadow effect you see in a black and white film noir movie.

The shadows hit my face and the wall and stacked all the way down toward the floor like a ladder composed of light.

I had spent so much time thinking about it, reading about it, and now, I finally could begin. I was nervous that I wouldn't be able to do it "right". I felt this bubbling anxiety clenching my throat. Meditation seemed so mystical and mysterious, like something only sadhus or monks might do, and now here I was, sitting in my room, wrapped in this white blanket, alone on a Thursday night. Could I really meditate on my own? Was I really skilled enough? Here I was, just a depressed teenager, sitting alone in my room on a Thursday night, wrapped in a white blanket like some wannabe guru.

Finally, I closed my eyes.

I took a deep breath and the air filled my lungs, cool and slightly musty. I gasped softly because just then a mandala materialized in the darkness behind my closed eyes. It was as vivid as a photograph, so clear and detailed that for a moment I wondered if I had somehow opened my eyes without realizing it. The image was shaped like a tunnel, but it wasn't smooth. Instead, it had a checkered pattern, like a black and white chessboard extending into infinity. In the center of the mandala was emptiness that faded into darkness.

I felt a very strong intuitive message that I should look down into the middle of this checkered tunnel. As I focused, I then noticed that it wasn't a smooth tunnel, but was blocky. The checkerboard pattern symmetrically created a round set of stairs, as if you could walk into this new dimension. My heart raced. Was this real?

As I increased my concentration, I felt myself being sucked down into this vision of a tunnel at lightning speed. The sensation was overwhelming, like flying and falling, hurtling through space and time. I was moving deeper, further down this tube, as if I were flying warp speed into another dimension, getting sucked deeper and deeper inside this portal. I tried to hold on but it but didn't last. Was I hallucinating? I felt a mix of exhilaration and terror, like standing on the edge of a cliff, knowing you are about to jump but not knowing if you'll fall or fly. I left behind my room, my problems, my very self. For a moment, I felt otherworldly, utterly, strange and alien yet energized. I wanted to stop this, but my soul craved more.

But this feeling of fear was too terrifying. Panic rising in my chest, freaking out, I popped my eyes open. I froze and didn't move off my meditation cushion.

What I saw next shocked me.

My heart was pounding so hard I could hear it in my throat. Was this how I was supposed to feel? After I calmed down, I looked around the room and noticed two odd things. The first was that I could see very large red and blue translucent objects floating all around my room. These objects appeared to be non-material and were moving through the walls like clouds moving across the sky on a windy day. The second thing almost impossible not to notice was light coming in from the window fading in and out. I don't know how but my entire field of vision went black. I couldn't see anything except darkness for a second, and then my vision would return. This happened for several minutes. Everything would go black, then return. I was too afraid to close my eyes again, and also too afraid to move. I wanted to get up and run to tell my father what had happened but what exactly would I say? Instead I just sat there in a semi-confused state, not quite sure what to make of it all, watching the colors pass by.

I continued meditating every day after that, but I soon realized this experience wasn't something that happened very often, and perhaps, it would never happen again.

I didn't tell my father about this experience. He and I rarely talked because my father didn't really know how to talk to me, only how to talk at me. He never asked me any questions, ever. If he didn't like something I did, instead of talking about it like a normal human being, he would angrily yell at me for a long time. For a man who never spoke, he sure did have a lot of things to say when he was angry. I never cried and he never apologized or told me he loved me. He became scared when I started mirroring him. I needed to stand up for myself against a man who only knows how to yell and only has the ability to communicate through anger. So, for the first time in my life, I decided I couldn't stay quiet anymore. After I began returning fire with fire, he could see that his verbal approach was now getting him in hot water and he didn't like it. He responded by increasing his intensity, but I could always match him in return. I was not standing up for myself; I was trying to survive psychologically. I felt like I was suffocating. Fear couldn't begin to explain how I felt about my father. I would just sit in my room waiting for him to burst in. When I opened my door, I did so slowly, quietly, so that it made no noise. He kept his door closed, so I'd quietly walk out into the kitchen, grab a snack, and tip-toed back to my room, feeling like I was in a mine field, slowly turning my door knob so that my father couldn't hear me. He had no idea the effect his behavior had on me. I had been a confident kid once. Now that kid was unrecognizable.

At that time in my life, I was also into reading books about aliens and out-of-body experiences. I tried to tell him about what I was into, but that was a huge mistake. He told me he was an alien, and he constantly criticized my interest in astral projecting because he suffered from paranoia, trying to scare me with made-up stories filled with his own biased fear. Sure, he probably thought he was being helpful in a pitiful sort of way. It was more annoying more than anything. He reminded me of that father who asked me with whom I wanted to live when I was only three years old, someone who was completely out of touch with reality and let his emotions carry him away. I never even really knew this was a type of emotional abuse I was going through until much later.

But at least we had meditation in common. He took it upon himself to give me very long lectures about meditation, never once asking me what I thought about what he was saying. It was always a one-sided conversation.

Around that time, we moved from Agoura Hills out into the San Fernando Valley. It was harder to meet up with my friends. I never learned what a healthy parental relationship looked like. I only saw my mom once a year for a week or two.

I began smoking weed to cope with my morbid depression. My mother finally convinced my father that I should meet with a therapist once every two weeks. That's when I met Nathaniel Branden, the psychologist. I needed to start healing, to clear out the dark cloud of confused depression and build self-esteem, but it seemed impossible while living with my dad. We fought all the time, and that kept opening up all the bloody, emotional wounds that never had a chance to heal. I began to feel suicidal.

I took naps all the time, maybe six times a day to escape from my perpetually depressed state mind. I knew I had to deal with my mental problems but I just didn't know how to do it. I couldn't handle it. So far meditation wasn't really helping.

Through Nathaniel Branden I learned about "the pillars of self-esteem" found in the practice of self-acceptance which at the time that seemed like a foreign language to me. To learn about it I read his books and took extensive notes, continuing my quest for sanity and spiritual insight.

I turned eighteen during my senior year at Agoura High School. In last year of school, I tried to feel normal, standing around during break time between classes. I had been outcast from the druggy clique—a situation that I was still okay with—but now I felt like a loser because I didn't belong to any clique at all. Since I had grown up in Miami, I didn't have any childhood friends in the area. At Agoura Hills High School, I changed friends about as fast as the carousel could spin.

No wonder that on my first day back, school already got on my nerves and put me down. I stood outside with the other students but didn't fit in with anyone, any group, anywhere. I just stood there by myself waiting for classes to begin.

The seniors hung out in the open quad closest to the gym and the parking lot. In the previous year, I had sat on the top of a hill under a tree with a group of punk girls. They listened to bands like *The Smiths* and *The Cure*. The girls were back, dressed like members of *The Suicide Squad*. Perhaps they wouldn't mind if I hung out with them again this year?

Adi, Kelly and Shelly had been my only real friends on the hill. Adi's skin was pale white and she dressed edgy smart with a hint of "you better not fuck with me." Shelly dressed like she was in a Pixar film and about to take over the world. Her parents were Japanese and she was the loudest girl in the group. She wore black and white striped leggings, purple thigh high army boots, and purple lipstick. Her t-shirts were usually primary colors, like yellow with green trim around the collar, and a brand logo on her wide chest.

I wandered up to the hilltop and was happily surprised by the girls greeting me with smiles, glad that I had joined them in social rebellion again. I wore baggy pants, multiple necklaces, leather wristbands. I wasn't hanging with the stoner crowd anymore, so I fit in just fine.

"I like this Johnny Depp thing you got going," Adi said.

There were a few other girls in the circle who I didn't talk to as often. Kelly was also quiet and shy, but she always smiled at me and was super nice. I ended up going to a party at her house up in the hills. I liked her soft and squeaky voice.

Mostly, though, I talked to Adi and Shelly, who both had a crush on me. At least, I knew Adi did, so Shelly probably backed off, and maybe Kelly did too. I think Kelly and I would have been the best match. I didn't date any of them, though. We were just friends. Years later, I realized that I had many opportunities to hook up with Adi, but was too innocent to realize it at the time. She never made the first move and maybe figured I wasn't into her.

Adi told me not to work out or get too muscular. She smiled, winked, and leaned in close. "Too many actors all look the same," she said. "Stay the way you are. Cutting edge." She wanted me to stay retro.

Adi was totally cutting edge. She listened to *Jane's Addiction* before class on her portable Walk-man and dressed like she didn't care what all the jocks and preps thought about her with her black lipstick and bleached white hair. She wore black fishnets that were torn and Doc Martins. She inspired me to start dressing differently, too. I started wearing suspenders, much to the ridicule of the jocks. I guess there was some gossip about it. People also gossiped that I smoked cigars, which I never did.

I guess these people imagined me sitting around in my suspenders and smoking my fat cigars, cursing: "Fuck the jocks and their square ass mentality."

Actually, I wore suspenders because I had lost my belt, and without it, if you tried or really wanted to, you could have looked down my pants. Whatever. If I had lived in the time of the Old West, I wouldn't have been the banker; I would have been the Outlaw who rides into town, not thinking about settling down. I didn't belong. I wasn't going to marry my high school sweetheart and live behind a white picket fence. I was going to ride out into the wild country, face off with death and live to tell the tale. Yeah, that's actually how wearing suspenders made me feel. Nobody else wore suspenders. And maybe I actually looked more like a clown in a circus show, but I didn't care.

A few weeks after school started, I leaned against a guardrail on the walkway near the hill with the only tree in the quad, which was the only place the punk clique hung out. The jocks hung out on the benches, and the skaters hung out by the lockers, everyone separated by choice.

Shelly walked over to me, smiled, and said, "Hey, how's it going?"

"Okay, I guess."

"Adi told me that you like to draw and you're into comic books." She put her elbows on the railing I was leaning against and looked up at me. I could see the earring that used to pierce her lip had been removed.

"I do," I admitted. "You like anime, right? I've watched a few anime."

"Really? Which ones?"

"*Sword Art Online*, and I like that one with the track suit. God, what's it called? *Nora...*"

"*Noragami*."

"Yeah, that one," I said. "I liked how every time God's disciple did something bad that bad thing would also appear as a purple blight on the body of the God. Like he was taking his bad karma away by absorbing the blight."

"That's a funny thing to like about *Noragami*."

"I mean, when I learned how to meditate and got initiated by my Guru, it felt like he literally took a load of karma off my back," I explained. "I felt so much lighter, like he took my blights away, just like in *Noragami*. I thought that was pretty cool. Considering the fact that gods live on the Astral Plane and aren't actually human."

"It's just an anime, though," Shelly said, awkwardly.

"Yeah, well, it has a lot of spiritual truth to it."

"You're really unique," she said, sarcastically, and rolled her eyes.

"Thanks, I guess." I didn't smile.

Shelly pivoted and walked back to her punk clique.

For a while, I stood there alone, waiting for the break to be over, when a beautiful Indian girl with long black hair and a gap between her two front teeth walked up and smiled at me. I'd never seen her before, but she looked gorgeous, even though she dressed like a tomboy with no make-up.

"Hi, what's your name?" she asked, beaming.

"Greg," I said, amused. "What about you?"

"Taj. I just transferred schools here from England."

"I transferred here from Miami a couple of years ago."

"Really," she said. "I knew we'd have something in common."

She looked back at a few of her friends who were looking at me, all smiling.

Taj had a wide smile, too, and a memorable laugh. She had the most beautiful eyes, dark brown, and her lashes were naturally long. I found myself hypnotized the longer she talked. Mostly, I was impressed by her confidence. She had a lot of charisma for a freshman in high school.

As we talked, Taj kept smiling at me, which helped me to smile more. Smiling was difficult because I was depressed. When she laughed, I also felt like laughing—that was strange for me, too. Ever since my bad acid trip, I had stopped laughing or smiling.

"My ex-boyfriend was such a jerk," she said.

"Oh, really?" I lost my smile.

I didn't want to hear about her ex-boyfriend, but she kept talking about how she hated him. I began worrying she would talk about me that way after we broke up. Yeah, I was thinking that the first time we met. I knew she wanted to date me by the way her friends kept staring at me and giggling, and how she kept talking and wouldn't leave. I liked her and I think she knew it.

A few weeks later, as predicted, I started dating her. She was my only real girlfriend in high school, a confident Indian girl who had just transferred to America from England. Before that, she had lived in South Africa. Her full first name was Tajal, but everyone called her Taj.

Technically, she was my second girlfriend in high school. My first was a Brazilian girl I dated over summer break in Miami Beach, much to my mother's disapproval. If my mom had lived in California, she wouldn't have approved of Taj, either. Taj dressed like a gangster—baggy pants, Adidas with fat laces, and an oversized plain navy blue t-shirts—but we got along well. She liked to listen to Stevie Nix and Snoop Dog. I liked rap, too, but I preferred Ice Cube. When I had lived in Miami, I liked rap. I was never into metal or rock.

Every day after school, I walked to Taj's house. She lived nearby, and I'd spend two or three hours there before it started getting dark and I had to drive home. Soon, I became good friends with her mother, Hema. Not too long after I had been hanging out at their house, Hema opened her daughter's bedroom door and discovered Taj and I kissing.

Taj shrieked, "Mom, get out!"

As expected, Hema gave us a long lecture and seemed upset. I sat there wondering what the big deal was and looked at Taj, who never showed any weakness, but at the moment, she was nervously looking over at me. Then, as if by magic, after thirty minutes, Hema calmed down, although still concerned.

"Greg, you have to keep this a secret," she said. "You can't tell Taj's father because he'll kill you."

I still wasn't taking her words seriously. I looked over at Taj, who nodded.

"He will literally kill you," Taj said.

I gulped and said nothing.

Taj's mother and I now shared a secret that brought us closer and strengthened our bond. Since my mom had now moved to Maine, I was missing a mother's guidance in my life. I adopted Hema to act as my new mother. She accepted the job.

Hema taught me how to cook Indian food and showed me her temple. She showed me how to apply the red powder to Lord Ganesh and Lord Shiva. She thought it was amazing that I knew about Indian culture and had an Indian Guru. She loved to ask me questions about meditation.

"I'm just so stressed out all the time, I should really learn to meditate," she said. "Do you think you could teach me?"

"Well, I can take you to learn from my teacher," I offered. "But I could teach you a simple method for now, if you like."

"Okay, teach me later, when we have time. I need to make dinner."

"Let me know," I said.

She often told me she loved my smile and that my eyes were sparkly and filled with light, probably because I was a good meditator. She had lost that spark herself.

Meditation practice helped me feel better when I was at school during the week for about three or four days. Then I would feel miserable again by Friday.

Taj didn't seem to mind that I was massively depressed, but she did mind that I was busy meditating all the time. Maybe I just hid my depression too well behind a social façade of a happy-go-lucky mellow dude. I wondered what I was doing in school anyway, because I certainly didn't want to be there.

CHAPTER VII

PAST LIFE RECALL

You might have spontaneously remembered something in a mysterious way, as if they were dreams happening to someone else. Maybe those memories are indeed yours, recalled from a past life you probably don't remember.

That happened to me when I skipped school with Sean Leahman. Sean was a wildly charismatic, boisterous surfer dude from Malibu. He had a lot of energy; joy seemed to be his second nature, but in a forced kind of way. He tried too hard to be spiritually correct. He wouldn't tolerate any negativity and he made sure everyone knew it. Jeff Grimm was his other best friend, and we all hung out together.

Sean was in my senior class in high school. Following problems in Malibu, he had to transfer into Agoura Hills. Here was another part time vagabond wandering into my life. I guess you could say I belonged to the vagabond clique in high school. Jeff was a hippie looking for a place to fit in. He was attracted to the mystic meditation wisdom talk I'd spit out on the quad, and the music I played in my car.

"Can I borrow some of your Indian classical music," he asked.

"Sure, I'll make you a mix tape," I smiled.

"You're like dressed in neon, man, while everyone else wears black and white. I'm feeling your spiritual vibes man," Jeff said.

"Thanks bro," I nodded. "Meditation is the shit."

My friends were either kicked out of school or had been kicked out of another school and newly arrived, like Sean or Taj. Oh, yes Taj also had a troubled academic history back in England. My senior year was the first time that friends of mine didn't get kicked out of high school.

Jeff, Sean and I formed our own retro hippie surfer clique. Sean was the major surfer but we all grooved cohesively. I surfed some as well, and carried my background into a colorful Indian Miami Vice resonation. Jeff was breaking out of his preppy phase, and letting his hair grow out.

Halfway through this year, Sean and Jeff joined my group under the tree up on the hill. The girls welcomed them with open arms. Sean especially caught Adi's attention, and they began seeing each other.

"So, do you like him?" I asked.

"He's just my boy toy," Adi grinned.

"Must be nice."

Adi stretched, opening her arms, displaying some kind of rash.

"What happened?"

"Sean and I were rolling around in the grass and it turned out to be poison oak."

"Yikes. Looks like it hurts."

"My arm just itches really bad."

Adi and I sat down on the hill and ate our lunch. Shelly was yelling something as usual. There was another cute

Armenian gothic girl there too. I thought she was attractive but never did or said anything because I had already started dating Taj. I felt like my life could fall apart at any moment and I needed Taj's infectious cheerful personality. But Taj was just a freshman so our schedules didn't always match.

Sean walked up. His shoulder length hair had nearly turned into dreads from lack of washing and salt water. He smiled and greeted Adi with a "What's up?"

"Hi, Sean," Adi smiled back, but then got up and sat with Shelly.

Sean wore leather sandals. If it weren't for the surfer shirt, you would think he was a hippie who smoked weed all the time. He lay down next to me on the grass.

"What a beautiful day!" he said, with a smile. He closed his eyes.

"Did you hear about the mandatory pep rally?" I asked.

"That blows." He added in a whisper, "Wanna ditch?"

"Totally."

When the bells rang, the other girls stood and put on their backpacks. We did the same. I looked at Sean and he nodded. He followed me down the hill.

"See you guys later," I called out to the girls.

"You're not coming with us?" Adi looked bummed.

"We're ditching."

"Fuck school!" Sean yelled.

That got Shelly and a few of the other girls to hoot and holler.

Sean and I walked quickly across campus toward the parking lot.

"So, tell me more about this meditation shit," Sean said. "Did you meditate over the summer?"

"Sure did," I said. "It was awesome. I hung out with a friend of mine, Bryan, and we were meditating like five hours a day on Saturday. On Sundays, I'd go to this group out in the Valley and get in two hours. I was going deep and feeling mellow."

"Right on. You're always mellow bro. I'll go with you next time."

"Any time, just let me know."

Finally, we walked into an area where we knew we wouldn't get caught and started up a hill.

"So, how do you do it?" Sean asked.

"You've got to have that beginner's mind," I said, taking my information from my groups and books. "Realize that only this moment exists. One time I was meditating, I had this vision of two fingers pointing to each other. The past and the future are both pointing toward *now*. When you're totally present in the moment, you can let go and surf the wave of life."

"Dope."

Sean waited by the side of my car as I walked around to the driver's side and opened the door. That year, I had a bright orange VW square back, after having crashed my forest green VW bug. I revved the old sputtering engine and we rolled out the school parking lot and on our way toward the Las Virgines Hindu Temple.

"So, what do you believe in, man?" Sean asked, casually. "Like would you call yourself Hindu or Buddhist? Fuck Christianity, that blind belief shit is so backward."

"I've developed my own way."

"Right on," he said. "Lay it out, bro. Hit me."

I told him how my belief system began when my mom told me about her spontaneous out-of-body experiences, about how I believed her stories and how they influenced what books I read and the questions I've been asking for the last five years—questions like what happens after we die.

"Out-of-body experiences are similar to near death experiences," I said. "Basically, they're the same thing, except in a near death experience you receive a welcome home party."

Sean laughed. "I like the sound of that."

"So, I began to see all these similarities," I said, "and one of the biggest ones I saw was where you go after you die. I mean, no one knows, right? No one comes back from the dead to tell us what happened."

"Unless they have a near death experience."

"Exactly," I said. "So, I got into reading books like *The Tibetan Book of the Dead*, but the book that really made it for me was Yogananda's *Autobiography of a Yogi*. In chapter forty-three, I think, his Guru resurrected like Jesus. And, you know, people haven't been able to stop talking about Jesus for, like, two thousand years. It's getting old. Yogananda's Guru resurrected about seventy years ago. So I trusted my gut feelings, making my own conclusions and testing them out."

"Like science class," Sean agreed. "You've gotta test out your theory."

"But unlike science, your laboratory is your personal experience," I said. "That's where scientists can go wrong. They discard personal experience because it's subjective. But that's all we have to go on when it comes to the inner science. So, what I've done is draw some conclusions that are wild. If I can prove them for myself, then that's what's true for me."

"What do you call yourself?" Sean asked.

"A spiritual practicalist."

"I dig it," he said. "It's spiritual because you're exploring the realms of spirit and a practicalist because you're testing it out. But is practicalist even a word, man?"

"Could also call it a spiritual pragmatist, whatever."

Sean rolled down his window, stuck out his hand and waved his hand out the car up and down, like a surfer riding wind.

"Yeah, so there is this invisible path to follow," I said. "I follow The Way. The Way is like the Tao. Do you know about the Tao?"

"Isn't that like an Asian religion?"

"I wouldn't call it a religion, even though it's a form of Buddhism. Lao Tzu boils down his wisdom to its essence. He wrote, "The Tao that can be spoke of isn't the Absolute Tao. The names that can be named are not the Absolute Names.""

"What's that mean?"

"He's talking about the name of God. It isn't spoken. So many different religions want to say I worship so and so, and if you don't worship the same God, then you're wrong. But God can't be confined to any one religion. You can give God a hundred different names. Call him Allah, or Krishna or Nirvana. Call her Goddess Tara, or the Holy Mother, or Ma Durga. No matter how many names you give her, you still can't speak the real name of God. The real name is literally unspeakable. Like the Tao. And when you give a name to it, that isn't it. Lao Tzu also said, 'My teachings are very easy to understand and very easy to practice, but no one can understand them and no one can practice them.' That's the path of The Way. You begin to understand something that nobody else understands and everyone thinks you're crazy. But how can they know that they don't know about what they don't know?"

"That's right on, man," said Sean. "We are 'practicalists' on The Way. But I don't like that word spiritual. It sounds like some New Age bullshit. That's our parents' generation."

"Yeah, man. What do you suggest then?"

"We just follow The Way. We don't define ourselves. Isn't that the whole point? You don't want to confine yourself to any one ideology but accept all religious paths as potential paths to the essence of Truth. No one's high, no one's low. We all have our place in the world."

"Right on, man," I said, smiling. I pulled up to a stop light after exiting the freeway. I hung a right and drove down a road, which dead-ended, and then hung another right and drove for half a mile. The Hindu temple was on the left.

I parked my orange VW below the temple. Normally, we would enter through the main entrance, but for some reason we went toward the closed downstairs door. Sean opened the door and entered first. I followed.

Sean walked in the temple on his own course, without any particular destination. I stood there and looked around the room we were in, becoming familiar with the unknown surroundings. I looked up and saw a quote from *The Bhagavad Gita*, VI: 30:

He who sees Me everywhere in all things and beholds everything in Me

Never loses sight of Me, nor do I ever lose sight of him.

He who sees me everywhere in all things.

In that moment, I was transported somewhere.

The vision hit me like a bolt of lightning, sudden and electric. One moment I was standing in a quiet Hindu temple off Las Virgenes Road, and the next, I was transported across time and space to some far off land, where I stood under a large tent, the kind you see during religious festivals. The scent of incense and flowers filled me as I found myself looking around at the people at the gathering. Where was I? Why had so many people gathered here?

Women in vibrant saris, reds, oranges, yellows and greens surrounded me, their bangles jingling softly as they moved. The dirt floor beneath my feet felt solid and real. A sense of profound peace washed over me, my mind slipping effortlessly into a meditative state. I began to realize that the people around me were from India because of the way they were all colorfully dressed. But what really amazed me is this sense of tremendous peace and the feeling that I was in the flow of life.

And, just as quickly as the vision had come, I was back, just standing below that sign in the Hindu temple, the vision had faded. I was left disoriented and breathless in the temple. I blinked, trying to reconcile the two realities.

The concept wasn't entirely foreign to me. My father had told me about his spontaneous past life recall, only he was transported back to Europe, planting the seed of this potential experience in my mind. But this... This felt different. More visceral. More real.

What was that? Was this a memory? Did I just recall a past life? It felt as if I were looking out of my own eyes, like I was standing in my own body, but living in a different place and time.

I glanced around, half expecting to find an answer. Instead I just saw Sean admiring a statue of a topless Hindu Goddess, oblivious to my momentary journey through time. I walked over to him and looked at the statue. It was grey stone, well crafted and I liked the woman's belly.

"I just had a trippy experience," I said, in a daze, my voice sounding distant to my own ears.

Sean turned, his wildly charismatic grin spreading across his face. "Yeah, this whole place is trippy."

I decided not to tell him what happened, unsure how to explain it all and not sound like some crazy person. How do you tell someone you might have just remembered a past life? Especially someone like Sean, who, despite his interest in our spiritual conversations, was tremendously opinionated and might think I was crazy.

So instead we explored the empty temple and continued discussing The Tao and what it means to be on The Way.

"It's written in such obscure language that everyday people can't conceptualize it as a religion," I said. "That's the point. It isn't a religion, it's a practice. We don't grasp onto concepts, but we have an open mind."

"No grasping, young grasshopper," Sean joked. "All right, if we're going to start our own thing, then what are some of the principles we follow?"

"The first thing is that we realize we live in a world of action," I decided. "We need to take action to have an experience. The second is this moment. There is nothing more important because this moment is all we really have. And, third, we are our own teacher. You are your own best guide. We believe in direct experience. Direct experience for us is scientific proof."

"Self-reliance is the only way to attain knowledge," said Sean. He smirked. "I like that idea, but I want to add something else. I'm making up a new word for it. I call it *Beingness*. Simply be and live your life. Beingness *is* knowledge. It's a state of being present in the moment. When you empty your head of all your whacky beliefs and ideas and simply be, that is The Way."

"Right on, brother," I agreed. "Give up all ideas of ego and just be."

"The ego is death!" he shouted. "Death to the ego!"

"And, lastly, all methods are just a means to an end, and not the end in itself," I said. "We don't want to glorify some technique and call it sacred or holy. What's sacred and holy is within."

We could say the words and we could think about them, but I'm not sure how well we understood them. Still, meditation itself seemed to be leading us to experiences we would never have encountered by ourselves. In the months ahead, Sean was initiated by a representative of Guru Sant Thakar Singh, and he saw a vision of the Master in a doorway of light, surrounded by darkness and holding his arms open wide.

During a meditation, Sean said the inner light blinded him for three hours. He couldn't see even when he tried to stand and walk around. Up until this point, I had never even thought that was possible — to be blinded by what you might see with your Inner Eye.

Sean and I would go night surfing sometimes, and I met his family, including his sister, Molly, who seemed to think I was pretty cool. As the weeks in the school year went on, though, my friend developed an anarchistic attitude and he disappeared for six days. His parents sent out a search and rescue party that cost them thousands. Another time, he drove through a tunnel with a car filled with friends. He believed that if he closed his eyes and had faith and trusted in the Supreme One, he would make it through the tunnel unharmed. He crashed the car and Sean dropped out of school so it was a tragedy that I lost my best friend.

Through this spontaneous vision I experienced with Sean and another friend of mine I didn't mention named Matt, I glimpsed fragments of past lives that have possibly shaped my current spiritual quest. These experiences have shown me that our spiritual goals and growth don't reset with each new life, but rather build upon the foundation we've already laid. I know most people in the west may not believe in this idea of living life after life.

But even for those who doubt the idea of reincarnation, the idea that our actions and choices are remembered throughout time, influencing future generations and shaping the world long after we're gone, offers a compelling metaphor.

Our actions echoing into the future, like seeds shaping lives beyond our own, planting forests of wisdom helping those who have not yet been born.

Then imagine the reverse was also true and the memories of our past lives were indeed sending messages to our future selves in order to enlighten our present life to the possibility of waking up. But why wake up? What wisdom was this that was arising from within, allowing me to remember my past life revelations?

CHAPTER VIII

SPIRITUAL BANK ACCOUNT

The more I meditated, the more I could achieve a steady level of concentration. The more I concentrated my attention, the less depressed I felt. Concentration was the key. Meditation seemed to cure my depression, something I considered almost impossible. When I could stop my thoughts, the depressing thoughts also disappeared. After a deep meditation I felt lighter, free of the doldrums. I didn't try to figure out why; I just enjoyed the relief while it lasted. But after a few hours the negative thoughts returned, along with the feelings of sadness and self-loathing. If you guessed that's the reason I became a meditation addict, you'd be correct. Concentration was my medicine — the practiced concentration focused within upon the essence of soul.

I also tried other solutions for depression, including seeing a therapist once a week, arranged my parents. My shrink, Nathaniel Branden, was well known as a psychotherapist and the founder of a self-esteem movement. He had written a book titled The Six Pillars of Self-Esteem, among several others. Branden had also been a lover of Ayn Rand. In the 1960s, he promoted her philosophy of Objectivism. In 1999, a movie was made about his affair with the famous writer, titled The Passion of Ayn Rand, starring Helen Mirren. Eric Stoltz played Branden. The film was based on a book written by Barbara Branden, the first of the psychotherapist's four wives.

I bought and read all of the man's books and practiced the psychological techniques he wrote about, mainly the method of being authentic and practicing self-acceptance and self-responsibility. I repeated affirmations like 'I accept myself here and now', but I couldn't find the peace that self-acceptance should bring. There were moments I seemed to realize a state of self-acceptance through the magic of continuous effort. I knew it was possible to achieve, but the recurring malaise of chronic depression kept creeping back in. Branden, then in his mid-60s, eventually gave up and said he couldn't help me. He even yelled at me for talking too quietly. We ended our sessions with no sense of resolution. It felt like his ego was too big and he couldn't relate to a seventeen-year-old kid who was still looking for himself. He was like a father who just wanted to make you follow his unconvincing cold advice, without expressing the degree genuine compassion necessary for a licensed therapist.

I left therapy feeling like meditation would be the only answer.

I returned to The Bodhi Tree and browsed the shelves. I spoke to another customer about her out-of-body experiences. The woman explained that every action has its reaction. In her mind, we earned our suffering and rewards. She said angels granted the boons and demons brought us pain. The customer described these agents as fairy spirits from the lower sub-worlds in the astral plane, and that the spirit world is an inseparable reality in grand creation of the Universe.

"No good deed goes unpunished," she joked.

In the same year, I had my first out-of-body experience. It started with some speculation, wondering if I could wake up inside a dream to become lucid enough to stop the dream and escape out into the astral plane. That was my theory. How did I do it? I killed myself in a dream. I jumped off a cliff, and discovered I could leave my body, just like my mother.

In the dream, I was standing on the edge of what looked like the Grand Canyon, enjoying a beautiful sunset. I became lucid and remembered my idea to escape. Quickly, I dove off the cliff to my death. But I didn't die, of course. This was just a dream. Instead, I became aware of the space around my body. I couldn't really feel my body at all, but just the consciousness within myself. So, I tried to float out of my body. As my body lifted upwards, I could feel my astral body passing out of my physical body. It felt as if I were putting my face into a cold pool of water. Then I was stuck at my hips and struggled for a moment. I was able to push off something and I popped out.

Soon I developed a procedure called the Death Method, where I again dive off a cliff or climb up onto a roof and jump off. I would fall for a few seconds toward the Earth until I dove into the ground itself. The "death" instantly stopped the dream. I could sense I was in my body, but this time I sat up as fast as I could and realized I was "stuck" at my hips. I lifted my leg and pushed against the wall. I pushed myself out of my Physical Body. I knew I had finally gotten free from my body and a wave of joy washed over my body. I had finally entered the astral realm. Immediately, the first thing I did was fly around.

Then I saw my first ghost.

The ghost was grinning at me like a weird, impossible Cheshire cat. Perhaps this was a flashback, residue left over from the bad acid trip at Disneyland. I couldn't believe I had left my body. The ghost's mouth was right next to my face. I was scared, because I was surrounded by darkness, and there was this smiling thing right in front of my face. What was this? Was this my own face? Was it a ghost? It seemed to be attached to me. My fear of this situation grew, the darkness, this freaky smiling creature in front of me — I shot back into my body.

Once the experience ended, I was immediately aware of being back in my body. As frightened as I had been, I was also exhilarated. I knew I wanted to try again. But what the hell was that smiling thing? Aren't ghosts supposed to look scary? This thing seemed to be enjoying itself, which made it even freakier. What the hell was it?

The books I read reinforced my expanding ideas about the world beyond the one in which we normally exist. I found the work of Paul Twitchell, a writer on the subject of meditation and out-of-body experiences. He had a complicated history with Masters and Yogis, as well as Scientology. He created his own religion, too, known as Eckankar. As a teenager, though, I was interested in him because he discussed levels he would reach in the afterlife while he was still alive (he died in 1971 of a heart attack, years before I was born).

According to Twitchell, there are many different levels, which may be found in the spiritual universe of the afterlife, including the immediate astral plane that contains hundreds of thousands of worlds and many sub-levels. These might be divided into multiple heavens and hells. Then, as you rise through the levels, you reach God-like status, and arrive in the celestial realm of the Gods, also known as the mental or subtle realm, it is also called the causal universe. The seeds of all our actions remained here, and these seeds would one day sprout and form our new karma for a future birth. The causal universe, as so many of these types of books remind us, is millions of times larger than the astral world. This is where the Buddhist heavens, Buddha realms, and God-like realms exist, all ruled by mental powers. Surprisingly, this level is still affected by ego, and the Gods here are sometimes jealous of each other. They compete with each other, and although there isn't violence like in the physical world, there are mental-wars, cleverness, trickery, and non-violent manipulations so intricate we can't even begin to comprehend.

Karma exists there, and these Gods can fall from grace.

Beyond these regions is the super causal, or the infinite realm, which many understand as the final goal. According to Paul Twitchell, this realm is surrounded by a great void, an infinity of emptiness. Here, there is nothing. No bliss. Just emptiness, the universal mind in its purest state. Twitchell's books were teaching me about such places as the great void, the infinite world of truth, and the realm of pure consciousness, the ocean of life.

These things I read about reflected some of my other discoveries and expanded upon them. I concluded the right combination of meditation practices might just take me up through these different levels of heaven and into the higher realms. Now I was getting somewhere and discovering the answer to my childhood question of "Where do I go when I die?"

I didn't know it yet, but the practice of meditation would become a profound journey of self-discovery for me, one that held the potential to elevate my consciousness beyond the boundaries of the everyday world. It was a path I would embark on with fierce determination, driven by the desire to unlock the mysteries of existence and transcend the limitations of human death.

Meditation had already revealed its transformative power. It was not merely a mental exercise or a relaxation technique; it was a doorway to higher realms of consciousness that I had only heard about in the books I'd been reading. As I delved deeper into my meditation practice, I began to glimpse the possibility of ascending into the beyond.

The key, I realized, lay in the right combination of meditation practices. I had explored my father's meditation practice, focusing my attention on the present moment, and witnessing the breath and how it allowed me to become more aware. I had ventured into Zen meditation, experiencing moments of profound stillness and interconnectedness with the universe.

It was through this synthesis of techniques that I began to ascend into higher realms of consciousness. I found myself floating on the edges of what some might call heaven, a state of existence where peace, love, and bliss reign supreme. The boundaries of my ego started to dissolve, and I experienced a sense of unity with all that is.

Entry into these heavenly realms, the ultimate goal of many spiritual seekers, seemed within reach. It was a space of pure enlightenment and liberation beyond the cycle of suffering. In my meditative journeys, I touched upon the edges of Nirvana, glimpsing the possibility of a state of existence beyond pain and suffering.

As I continued to meditate, my understanding of life and death shifted. I realized that the answer to my childhood question, "Where do I go when I die?" was not to be found in some distant afterlife, but rather in the depths of my own consciousness. Through meditation, I discovered that the true nature of existence transcended the physical realm, and I was on a path to explore these higher realms more fully.

In those moments of deep meditation, I felt as though I were on the cusp of a profound revelation, a journey that could take me even further into the mysteries of existence. The combination of dedication, exploration, and the right meditation practices had opened up a divine door of possibility. It was a journey I was willing to undertake, for I had come to understand that the answers I sought were not out there in the world, but within the boundless expanses of my Self. However, as distinguished from my own Self, or soul, I couldn't escape the idea that my mind and its conception of this world didn't actually exist. It was just hanging around, haunting me like a ghost.

Looking inside myself for truth and sanity through meditation didn't stop me from going outside, however. I enjoyed some of the best times of my life as a teenager riding waves in the great wide open, at the edge of the physical continent and the awesome liquid expanse of the Pacific Ocean. I had a blast surfing with Sean and Jeff.

We'd go in the summer and during the school year, even in winter. The water was frigid. We wore wetsuits. The adrenaline from catching waves pulsed through our blood. Looking down off a ten foot crest and dropping into the surge, half blind with water spraying in your face, was for thrill seekers hip to that fathomless power, not the faint of heart.

One day Jeff, Sean, and I lay on the beach in Malibu, basking in the warmth of the sun after surfing. I decided to tell my friends about experiences I had at the Monroe Institute, an education center·back east using technology to explore consciousness, founded by the author a book my mother had given me to read.

"Dude," I said, "you won't believe what I did last summer. I've been trying to have an O.B.E. experience."

"A what," Sean repeated. He had that typical skeptical look he often exhibited, like he was focused on something more important and I had just interrupted his train of thought.

"You know, out of body experiences. I listened to these sounds that put you in a deep sleep state that allows you to project out your own body."

"Greg, you are so weird man," Sean shook his head.

"Sounds cool," Jeff retorted

"I don't know anybody like Greg," Sean said. "Greg is always so laid back and chill."

"Maybe it's 'cause he's out of his body?" Jeff chimed in. We all laughed.

"How do you know this shit is real bro?" Sean asked.

"Many people who have had near death experiences in hospitals are able to see things happening in the operating room that they are later able to prove when they are brought back to life. They saw things happen that they never should have known about because they floated out of their body and watched the whole thing from the ceiling. There's actually been a lot of research done by doctors and cardiologists and hypnotists. The afterlife is nothing new."

"You think having a near death experience is similar to having an OBE?"

"Yeah, maybe." I paused, looking out across the water at a crashing wave and saw a surfer bail into the white foam and swallowed by the ocean. "I thought it was kind of boring at first. I mean, who wants to lie down and listen to some static noise for an hour, right?"

Jeff raised an eyebrow, "So, you actually did this or something?"

"It was my mom's birthday present," I nodded. "I got a discount for being a student. So I flew out to Faber, Virginia last summer to go do the Gateway program at the Monroe Institute. You stay for about a week and we'd do 5 to 7 sessions every day. And after the third day you start having some interesting experiences. It was wild. They've got this ten foot crystal you can meditate on."

"That's cool," Jeff looked at Sean for some sort of response.

"Sounds insane. So, what really happened their bro?" Did you see anything?" Sean knocked his long wet hair out of his face as he sat up, intrigued. He then brushed the sand off his shoulder but had trouble getting it off because he was still soaking wet.

As I settled into the hot sand, my toes wiggling to get comfortable, I tried to find the words to explain my unusual experience. "So, the Gateway Voyage is a program where they use a technique they call Hemi-Sync. They gave me headphones and played music using binaural beats — that's two separate tones of slightly different frequencies going into each ear that would synchronize in my brain hemispheres. The process induced an advanced altered state of consciousness that takes most meditation pros years to achieve. It's an ultimate shortcut to deeper states in meditation. I could feel the energy from the trees, from nature. Mostly I was meditating."

"At the Monroe Institute, they taught us how to use these relaxation techniques to explore deeper states of consciousness they called focus levels, similar to self-hypnosis. You start from simple relaxation count down techniques to full blown out of body experiences in less than a week. It was epic."

"Sounds epic," Sean nodded, fully interested in what I had to say now.

"You have no idea, it was like I was on this journey, discovering powers and abilities I never knew I had. I had visions. I saw things. My mind was giving me messages that I had to decode."

"So what vision did you have?" Sean asked.

"Mostly flashes of images that didn't really make sense. But I saw a crystal clear bunny rabbit. It was forty foot tall, standing in a field of grass with a thin row of trees behind it. It was all lit up with spot lights."

"Weird," Sean snorted.

"What did that mean?" Jeff asked.

"I'm not sure. But my Chinese zodiac is a bunny rabbit so maybe it has something to do with me. A lot of times your experiences in the astral world are symbolic, like dreams, so you need to interpret them."

Jeff looked at me with curiosity. "But how does it work exactly? What's so special about these sound frequencies your listening to?"

I thought for a moment, searching for the right words to describe the sensation. "Hemi-Sync creates this kind of relaxation or this resonance in my brain, and it helps your brainwaves fall into the sleep state. My brain was buzzing with vibrations and totally relaxed. And when that happens, your mind becomes more receptive to seeing visions, and entering higher levels of focus. It's like conscious dreaming, like you have a mental key that unlocks the doors to your third eye, man. You just have to stay present and not try to judge or conceptualize what you see because then the visions will stop."

Sean leaned back again, taking in my words. "So, you opened your third eye? Isn't that dangerous?"

"Not really," I replied. "It's like an inner adventure where you explore a new universe, see visions, interact with spirits, and awaken a new spiritual side of yourself. I don't know. Maybe I'll never be the same again. But it was incredible. I felt like I was connecting with a deeper part of myself, and it brought me a sense of inner peace and self-awareness that I'd never experienced before."

I remembered how the sun continued to warm our bodies and we took off our wet suits. As the three of us lay there, looking out at the ocean, I remember feeling tremendous gratitude for all the beautiful sunny days in California. My depression had been replaced in that moment and I remembered that, because it was a rare occurrence for me to actually feel happiness. And Sean was part of that happiness, but now he was gone.

"So what got you interested?" Jeff asked, "I mean, I've never heard anyone talk about this before."

"After my mother told me about her O.B.E. Experiences, I became terrified of death. I had no idea where I'd go after I died, but I wanted to know."

I kept looking for clues. I drove over the hills into Beverly Hills and found my way to The Bodhi Tree bookstore, where I picked up a magazine with an ad that featured a photo of a Guru from India. At home, I had continued to read the Autobiography of a Yogi. I re-read the excerpt I summarized in chapter four, where Yogananda discussed how his teacher reappeared after his death, just as Jesus did. I put down the book, picked up the magazine and called the number offered in the ad. I found out that the group held free public talks on Sundays.

The next Sunday, I drove to the meditation center in North Hollywood, which was run out of the house of a nice older woman named Pat. She had a southern twang and told me the group planned to show one of the Guru's videos. Pat told me they were having food after the video and that I was welcome to stay. There were about eight people listening to the talk given by a Guru from India. It disappointed me that he was not there in person. While I watched I began to feel confused. The guru I was listening to said that once you have a guru, you should be faithful to your guru. I suddenly felt as if I was being unfaithful to my father's guru. Then I suddenly felt ill. The feeling came on quickly so I stood to leave. But the man in the kitchen said he had some good Indian food that was spicy and good for illness. I looked at the food and it looked delicious so I sat back down and finished watching the talk.

After the video I felt better. Everyone filed out of the meditation room and into the cramped kitchen for the potluck lunch. I happily filled my paper plate with the variety of Indian dishes. Chairs had been pushed aside in the meditation room so we could sit on the floor and eat together. I chose a spot away from the others, off by the back wall where the sun was shining though sliding glass doors. Bright rays warming the side of my face, I saw someone sitting alone outside, calmly and contentedly eating at the patio table. But because I was sitting alone, I felt a bit insecure, or even inferior for a moment. I soon ignored the uncomfortable feeling, realizing that no one was there to judge me.

As I savored the Indian cuisine, I gazed at four or five colorful geometric paintings that resembled mandalas hanging on the walls. They conveyed an abstract spiritual essence, reminding me of visions I've had meditation. Incense and Indian flute music playing in the other room contributed to the relaxed atmosphere. Pat, John D. and Bryan, came over with their plates of food, introduced themselves and sat down on the floor next to me.

"It's unusual for someone your age to be interested in meditation," Bryan said looking at me with curiosity, noticing I looked young.

"That's cool Greg," John grinned. "How'd you find out about our center?" He seemed a little older than me but not by much. John wore a Grateful Dead T-shirt, had wavy long black hair. He leaned his arms back, in no rush to eat and kicked his feet out into the sunlight.

"Well, my father and mother met at a meditation center," I said, "So I've been around it my whole life. But recently I've been interested in how life after death relates to meditation. So, when I saw your ad, I was attracted to come check it out." I didn't mention that I was bummed that the actual teacher wasn't here.

Pat nodded. I asked, "Who are the three Indian men pictured on the wall? I've never seen these teachers before."

Bryan pointed to one of the figures and said, "This is Sant Thakar Singh, our current living teacher. He continues the teachings of his Master, Sant Kirpal Singh, who left the body in 1974. Kirpal Singh was the beloved teacher of Sant Thakar Singh, and Sant Sawan Singh had been the teacher of Kirpal."

My curiosity piqued even further. I marveled at this legacy and the meditation practice passed down over several generations. As we ate, I felt compelled to learn more about the teachings of Sant Thakar Singh, and the lineage of spiritual masters. Little did I know at that moment how this encounter would set in motion a spiritual quest of massive proportions that would stay with me for the rest of my life.

As I savored my last bite of the delicious Indian food, Bryan pointed out that the appellation "Sant" means something like Saint, or a human being who has attained the highest spiritual enlightenment, and who has dedicated his life to spreading this knowledge to anyone interested in learning about it. The fact that they taught this meditation for free impressed me. They explained that real Saints never charge, because they are not interested in personal gain. Finding or realizing God is everyone's birthright and should be offered freely.

"Finding God," I said, "Is that even possible?"

Bryan asked for my thoughts about it, but I found myself unable to answer. There was a peaceful vibe in the room that induced my mind to slow down. Maybe Bryan was just trying to be informal in order to relate to a guy like me dressed in baggy jeans, Adidas sneakers with fat shoe laces, and an XXL "My Crazy Life" shirt drawn by Mike Shinoda. But Bryan kept cracking jokes and talking in this funny laid back tone.

"Bryan's rap went like this: Okay, let me break it down for ya. Life begins with a single cell. That cell in the womb transforms from a tiny speck to a full-blown, complex human being. Just like how God became many, creating an infinite universe."

"The big bang," I said.

"It's like a divine symphony, orchestrating every step of the process. It's our karmic destiny to meet our creator. It's our soul's destiny," he continued.

Bryan started "droppin' knowledge" about how God created the world, and he wanted to know "what's popping in my head." Everyone in the group was amused.

"Life is about transformation, whether it's in the mother's womb or about getting this Indian food in my belly," Bryan said, laughing even harder as he dipped some naan bread into his saag paneer. "Wow, that's delicious! I think I just experienced God realization! This is what being connected to the universe is all about!" He exclaimed as he took another bite. I laughed, and then everybody was laughing. I never had so much fun talking about meditation. Bryan seemed like he knew how not to take life too seriously.

"So what's the real point of this meditation practice?" I asked.

"Oy vey, this kid is full of questions!" Bryan explained. The group laughed again. "It's hard to grasp everything all at once, but remember this essential point, meditation is a practice. In order to fully understand it, you've got to experience it, and once you go inside to see, you can't un-see. Like John's dance moves."

"Hey now, that's not fair," John laughed. "I challenge you to a dance off."

"All right, relax tough guy. I'm just making a point," Bryan joked.

"At my expense," John said, playfully sarcastic.

"Meditation is funny, like a paradox," Bryan continued. "Would it be farfetched to imagine trying to find stillness in the midst of a dance party?"

"That would be difficult," I agreed.

"I've tried," John added. "It's possible. But you got to surrender to the music."

"You sound like you've been smoking something," Bryan joked. The group laughed but John didn't.

Bryan continued, "But seriously, Meditation isn't always easy. It's like you're reaching for that silence within, but when you close your eyes you find a disco party poppin' in your head."

"I get that you got to silence your mind. I've meditated before," I said. "But what I'm getting at, or asking about is what's the deeper meaning or the grand plan? Is it possible to see God?"

"Good question bro," John chimed in.

"You're skipping from point A to Z. Are you sure you're ready for the answer?"

I didn't respond.

"The grand plan is unchangeable permanence. It's about divine intelligence my man, that calm center of far reaching expanded intelligence that only comes with grace," Bryan said.

"That's why we need to follow the instructions of the spiritual guide, and meditate. Grace doesn't come for free," John chimed in. "God helps those who help themselves."

That afternoon, Bryan focused on bridging the gap between the spiritual and scientific. He said that meditation is the practical and scientific method to become one with God. What's more, it started to sink in that I needed a spiritual guide, just like Yogananda had Sri Yukteswar's help. I am not clear why, but I never really felt my father's guru could direct me to higher awareness. I just didn't feel that pull.

"It makes sense right?" Bryan asked. "If you want to learn history you go to a history teacher. Meditation's no different." Feeling an irresistible compulsion, I lost any remaining doubts, like thinking there was something wrong or weird about learning meditation from a guru who happened to wear a turban. Americans are led to believe meditation groups are cults or something untrustworthy. But we shouldn't let a few bad apples spoil the bunch. The teacher-student relationship has existed for ages.

Bryan explained that we're lucky to be alive, and that the human body is the essential vehicle for realizing higher consciousness. Beyond the five physical senses, and the ghost mind, the mind that doesn't really exist, lies a sixth sense, an inner window. Once it's opened, I learned that I could find spiritual planes I never knew existed, through the astral and deeper into the great beyond, all the way to the soul's true home. This was also what I had concluded from all my reading.

Bryan went on to offer a systematic explanation of spiritual concepts, including how inner light can be perceived through the sixth sense or a third eye, and how human beings can clear karma by meditating on spiritual sound, as defined in Indian terms, Shabd, which means an "unstruck" sound heard within and vibrating throughout the cosmos. He explained that karma means action and reaction, as a consequence of our thoughts, words and deeds. Everyone has a storehouse of karma, good and bad alike, to be unpacked throughout the lifespan. The accumulated karma, increasing by the day, keeps us tied and bound to the physical world. We could reincarnate over and over again until the debt is paid — impossible to pay off without the help of a qualified meditation guide.

I opened up about my research into the spiritual planes and discussed books about life after death and how I had realized there were different levels. I had gone to a spiritual convention center event in down town L.A. and talked to someone who used to be a member of Eckankar and said he could help me to go into the astral plane. I had just sent him a check a few days ago.

"Oh, that's too bad. We teach for free here," Bryan said. "Have you read any of Paul Twitchell's books?"

"The Tiger's Fang," I said. "I liked the journey through the astral and causal planes, and beyond them to the black void."

"Oh, I can tell you it is true," Pat said. "I've been there."

"What?" I said somewhat surprised by her comment. I had only read about it but Pat was claiming she had actually been there. "What do you mean?"

"Dear, I've seen that great void," Pat said. "I was taken there by Paul Twitchell himself in an out-of-body experience. I used to be a member of Eckankar."

"Would you mind telling me your story," I asked. I

couldn't believe it; I was talking to someone who actually reached this rare inner region.

She briefly outlined her inner journey. Once during meditation, Paul had guided her through the inner spiritual regions. She held back on describing much about what she saw and just said Paul had led her along until they reached a great impassable black expanse. It was rumored that after entering that dark chasm of infinite depth, many unguided spirit travelers got lost couldn't find their way back out.

"What was it," I asked.

"It was the great void," she said. But more importantly, Paul told her that the void was as far as he could take her — all the way to that barrier of the great void but not beyond. She added that neither he nor his followers could gain access to the purely spiritual regions beyond that darkness. Bryan Thomas chimed in to tell me that Paul Twitchell used to be a disciple of Sant Kirpal Singh (who had been Sant Thakar Singh's Guru). Bryan said Twitchell claimed to have had visions of Kirpal Singh speaking to him at home, and that he wrote down what the saint told him. He then wrote the book, The Tiger's Fang, and asked Kirpal if he would help publish the book through his organization in India. The Master had not only denied that request, he had told him not to publish it at all.

Twitchell went outside the organization and published the book anyway. He then appropriated the Guru's methods — the light and sound meditation practice — and formed his own spiritual organization called Eckankar. Twitchell never publicly acknowledged his initiation by Kirpal. Paul just made up his own names for the different aspects of the meditation and even changed Kirpal's name to Shams Tabriz (a middle eastern saint and the poet Rumi's spiritual teacher) or something similar.

The public gathering at Pat's house was about to end and people began cleaning up, putting their shoes on and going home. Bryan Thomas said he could teach me the light and sound meditation if I agreed to become vegetarian. I was already vegetarian, no problem. I had no clear idea at the time about how lucky I was to be receiving this blessing.

After settling down in the quiet comfort of a cozy lounge chair, Bryan began to teach me the Light and Sound meditation method. He assured me that regular disciplined practice would bring greater results.

"Do not, however believe my words on blind faith," he said. "Follow the instructions to the best of your ability and see the results for yourself. Our lineage emphasizes practical experience. Sant Mat is a spiritual science and not a religion per se. Test it out first and then decide if this is something worth pursuing."

Bryan went on to review and add to everything he had discussed earlier, including aspects of the spiritual life style including the principle of "ahimsa," or non-violence in thought, word and deed, and the importance of chastity.

"Okay Greg, you see, this meditation you are about to learn can technically be classified as yoga. And what is yoga? Most Americans might think it only meant stretching exercise, but in Hindi it literally means union."

"So yoga is a type of meditation practice?"

"Exactly, Yoga is the most sacred practice passed down throughout the ages in India. There are various branches of meditation practice. But their aim is one and the same. The goal of meditation is to become one with the divine.

"To give it a name, this yoga is called Surat Shabd Yoga. Surat means attention or focus, and Shabd is the holy sound or Word. Sound meditation, or Shabd Yoga, is a process of merging or absorbing our individual consciousness into supreme oneness coming through the Word, through the inner Sound. Basically, the path to the One is through oneness. It's all about realizing that deep within your being, God perception is not only possible, but also easy to do. Even a child could practice the sound meditation."

"If God is perceived within this sound, then all we need to do is listen?" I asked.

"Oh, you're smart. By becoming one with the Sound, we win the game. It's like having a hotline to the big boss upstairs," Rich laughed.

"Can you explain what the Sound is? Is it an outer sound you actually hear?"

"Shabd is not an external sound coming to your ears but spiritual a sound heard within. Meditation on the inner sound will burn your inner barriers, your walls in the form of the deep impressions we've collected over the ages on the astral body, and the karmas holding us down in a never ending cycle of reincarnation. This prepares you to fly up to God. The inner Sound will lead you to higher states of awareness, thus granting you access to higher realms you never knew existed. Along the way you might sometimes experience something blissful, coming a deep well and source of infinite and abundant love, and be intoxicated by it. This divine melody is always there, waiting for your mind to just shut up and listen."

"How do I listen to it?" I asked.

"I'll teach you in a minute. So as we meditate, try to get all still and silent—that's when you'll start to hear that inner sound. It's like tuning in to your favorite radio station, where the signal gets clearer the more you focus. Here's where it gets very interesting. As you dive deeper into meditation and forget about the outside world, the sound draws nearer and eventually comes from above."

"Above?"

"It's permeated through the entire universe but to hear it, we must find it from within. It's like the inner heart beat that kicks off the universe's most epic track, you feel me?"

I laughed.

"The adepts of Shabd Yoga have always said that this original sound created the universe. It is the subtle fabric of the universe, the divine energy that exists within every atom of creation. You can realize this someday if you meditate regularly. That's the sound of the All-Conscious creator of the universe, the ultimate jam, the divine music that connects us to the cosmos and our life line that will lead to our final escape beyond the cycle of reincarnation."

I found it paradoxical what Bryan taught me next. He was teaching me some details using almost the same exact language that I had read Paul's book, *The Tiger's Fang*. There was too much synchronicity going on here. It seemed almost by design that I had read that book a week prior, and so I took this as a sign that I was supposed to be here, and had to learn this no matter what.

"Finding a solution to the question of where I going after death, it's important to me? And I think this is the answer."

"Whoa man, you just gave me chills. So do you agree with everything so far?"

I also took my first steps towards practicing self-acceptance that day, also accepting that I was improving my strategy to solve the riddle of unhappiness. Meditation seemed to promise the answers. I wasn't about to let myself be controlled by fear.

"I agree," I nodded. I was ready to start standing up for myself against my father's aggression. Some people might think I was crazy, starting a fight with my dad over something as fleeting as meditation. But isn't life all about going on an epic quest, facing formidable obstacles, and conquering the impossible. Hell yes, I was doing this!

The casual discussion ended and Bryan switched gears and went into formal instructions on both the inner seeing and inner hearing practices. To continue, I had to make commitments, one being to refrain from discussing all the details about the meditation method to anyone. I can relate here some aspects of the Light and Sound meditation process for general interest and inspiration. I need to emphasize, however, that to learn this practice properly, only an advanced spiritual adept who has reached the final stage of enlightenment, or an authorized representative of such soul, can safely help the seeker receive the transfer of spiritual current necessary establish the inner links to the beyond.

Here are some general aspects that Bryan related to get me going on this pivotal boost to my spiritual progress.

"The process of withdrawal of the sensory currents is the first step towards detachment from physical reality, and this is achieved through both physical and mental relaxation and stillness.

"With eyes closed sit fully relaxed, and be a silent witness. Just look into the darkness in front of you without any strain or tension. Look upward, focusing your gaze and attention above and between the eyebrows. This is the third eye or inner window where you wait for the light to appear. Try to remain as still as possible."

"Look into the darkness at as small a space as possible, with a penetrating gaze. Until all the outgoing faculties are inwardly focused, the spirit doesn't gain strength to go up The goal is to maintain single-minded attention, so all worldly thoughts vanish and your consciousness is automatically drawn upwards into the spiritual realms.

"Think of meditation like stepping into the world of 'The Matrix.' Did you see that film?"

"Yeah, I loved it."

"In the same way that Neo unplugged from the Matrix, we are unplugging from our mind. When you meditate, it's like when Neo said, 'There is no spoon.' In meditation, you realize that there is no mind, no self, only the present moment exists."

"That sounds deep," I said.

"It's a journey within, a path to enlightenment, where the 'spoon' was never real to begin with, and the mind doesn't really exist, it's just a ghost with no substance."

"So if the mind is just a ghost, does that mean who I think I am is not real?'

"Those answers will come to you in meditation. "

What is sound meditation? The Sound is the subtlest manifestation of energy and is in fact consciousness itself. It is the primordial manifestation of God underlying the Universe, as stated in the New Testament of the Bible in the first chapter of John: "In the beginning was the Word, and the Word was with God, and the Word was God." All things were made by this Sound according to many different religious texts. Most followers of those religions don't fully understand the meaning and essence of Word God and have lost sight of the practical spiritual implications. The 'Word' is not spoken to crowds; only a handful knows it in silence.

"When you meditate on the Sound you will naturally become absorbed into it, the body and mind achieve perfect rest while the soul—your consciousness—gains the purity and strength to eventually ride the waves of the Sound. It will eventually take you through and beyond spiritual regions within, until the soul eventually reaches its true home in the lap of God, the ultimate goal of the soul on the fifth and highest spiritual region or plane, called Sach Khand by the lineage of saints. An adept of Shabd, or the Sound, guides and protects you on the way." Bryan concluded.

Afterwards, we meditated for two hours I asked, "Would it be cool if we meditated another hour?"

Bryan and I continued silently into the night for another hour and stopped after it had gotten dark.

"No one's ever asked me to meditate longer before. If you want to meditate next weekend, let me know." Bryan wrote down his number and said good night.

The experience left me feeling much closer to reaching enlightenment and I was eager to explore this spiritual journey further. I believed I found the right practice that could take me through the astral plane and into the higher realms of pure bliss, akin to Nirvana. On the drive home, I became super excited, because I believed I had finally found the answer to what I'd been seeking. I couldn't contain my excitement as I rushed home to share my new-found knowledge with my father.

As I walked through the door, my enthusiasm was palpable. I greeted my dad with a bright smile, eager to share the details of the light and sound meditation.

But when I opened the door to our Agoura Hills apartment, my excitement quickly turned to apprehension when I saw the look on my dad's face. He was clearly not pleased with how late I was coming home, and his irritation only grew as I began to excitedly explain the new meditation group I'd just joined. It was like a Christian telling his parents he's converted to a different religion. I had unintentionally crossed a boundary that I hadn't even known existed.

My father had always been deeply devoted to his own spiritual practice, one that he believed was the only path to true enlightenment. He followed an Indian guru he revered as a "perfect master." A perfect master is one who has reached the highest stage of enlightenment and in my father's eyes; there was no room for alternative practices or different spiritual paths. To him, all other teachers were simply inferior.

As I nervously explained my experiences with light and sound meditation, my father's frustration only grew. He saw it as a betrayal, a rejection of the path he had laid out for me as the right path, and he couldn't accept it.

His anger was fueled by his unwavering conviction that his master was the real "perfect master." He believed that all other Indian gurus were lesser, their teachings flawed and incomplete. To him, there was no room for exploration, no possibility of finding truth in other spiritual practices. I was a rigid and dogmatic viewpoint that left no room for open-mindedness or tolerance.

I hadn't anticipated his reaction, and I was caught in a difficult situation. I had to think about the consequences of pursuing this new spiritual path despite my father's disapproval, or should I conform to my father's rigid beliefs to maintain harmony in our relationship. It was a decision that would shape the course of my spiritual journey and our relationship for years to come.

As the tense encounter with my father began to cool, I needed some clarity. So, I excused myself, claiming I was going to go for a walk, and made my way out of his apartment. I headed down the sidewalk and looked across the street. As I stood there, a sense of unease washed over me. The stillness of the night seemed to magnify every sound, every gust of wind, and the engine sputtering from the one car that lurched by. The parking lot, usually packed, was now a vacant sea of black asphalt, and the eerie emptiness made me ill at ease, and the vast empty space amplified my paranoia. I found myself standing alone, looking back over my shoulder feeling like someone was watching, listening to the echoes of my footsteps, which were amplified in the quiet of the night.

Was someone watching? Perhaps my father was, enshrouded by trees, disapproving and disappointed, looking out at me from the shadows? The thought freaked me out. I tried to shake it, but someone was out there watching. I could sense it in the pit of my stomach. The negative feelings my father had expressed had latched onto me like a slime mold that caused sickness and emotional decay.

With a quarter in hand, I dialed Bryan's number, my new friend who had introduced me to light and sound meditation and read the initiation instructions answered the phone. His voice was cheerful and a welcome relief from my previous interaction. "Hello," was all he said.

"It's me," I stuttered.

"Everything alright?"

As Bryan's voice came through the receiver, I quickly poured out my heart, telling him about my father's disappointment and the growing tension between us. Bryan remained calm and collected and listened attentively. Then, he asked me a simple yet profound question, "How do you feel right now after having meditated for two and a half hours?"

I paused for a moment, allowing Bryan's question to sink in. Closing my eyes, I took a deep breath and tuned into my own energy. Bryan was right. I felt a profound shift within me. After those hours of meditation, I felt lighter, more spiritually fulfilled, and freer than I had ever felt in my life. It was as if a veil had been lifted, revealing a deeper understanding of myself and the world around me. I felt a peace that transcended my current emotional turmoil and I immediately relaxed. I didn't care if someone was hiding in the bushes, watching me from across the street.

The contrast between the serenity I had experienced during my meditation and the current disagreement with my father couldn't have been starker. It was as clear as day. The choice I needed to make was apparent. I would continue to practice light and sound meditation, despite my father's disapproval.

Bryan's words of wisdom reminded me of the transformative power of meditation and the importance of staying true to my own spiritual path. My newfound sense of purpose and inner peace outweighed any external conflicts or disapproval from others. I knew that this path was the right one for me, and I was willing to face the challenges it presented, even if it meant going against my father.

With determination, I hung up the payphone and headed back to the apartment. Though the road ahead would certainly be challenging, I had found a source of inner strength that would guide me through the turbulent waters at home. My journey of self-discovery had only just begun, and I was ready to embrace it, even in the face of adversity. Everything for me had lead up to this moment.

On the weekends, I'd either hang out and meditate at Bryan's house. Taj never liked that I'd go off and meditate during the weekends, most likely because Bryan and I would try to meditate up to five hours a day. We didn't always get in five hours, but we tried. And, on Sunday, I would drive to the meditation group in Van Nuys and sit for two hours. So Taj started hanging out with some other guy on the weekend. I didn't know about this of course until later. I was engaged in something more meaningful.

Here, at last, through meditation, I was finding out the answers to my childhood questions. The answers could be found in meditation after all, but now, it was up to me to practice. I also continued reading in my spare time. I began meditating as much as I could. I would put in four to five hours on a Saturday, and then two to three hours on a Sunday and felt good, so by Monday morning, I felt much better, happier and less depressed.

Then, during the school week, my depression would return like a dark cloud that followed me around all day.

I'd repeat the process on the weekend, and turn down opportunities to meet with friends or hang out with Taj. I upped the amount of meditation, practicing five hours a day on the weekends, and I felt that inner peace as my mind stopped thinking.

I learned a major lesson—that after a long meditation weekend, I felt filled up and energized like a cup filled with water. I concluded that the body is like a cup and meditation was like water for the soul. The more you drink, the better you feel. You're accumulating this spiritual wealth and it has a direct effect on how good you feel. The more wealth you have, the better you feel. It was a pretty simple conclusion really. Meditate to feel happy. If you don't meditate, depression was unavoidable. That's what lead me to conclude that if I could find God, then I could overcome the depression permanently.

When graduation came, I didn't bother to pick up my diploma. The next day, I planned to drive up north.

As I packed my bags, I couldn't help but feel a sense of anticipation. It was as if I was preparing for a long journey. Each meditation session I'd put in over the past year, felt like small deposits into some invisible account. An account that didn't deal with the currency of dollars but in an accumulation of clarity and inner peace. How much spiritual wealth could I accumulate? And would it be enough to free me of this karmic burden of depression?

If I could find God, then I would have my solution. If I found Him, really found Him, I would be free from all this mental suffering at last. And maybe, just maybe, I'd discover that the real treasure wasn't something to be found, but something to be built, slowly and steadily, like interest accruing in a bank. I think I had just created a new concept, the existence of spiritual wealth. This concept is often overlooked or completely unknown. Meditation has long been talked about as a source of joy and fulfillment, but how does it work? I noticed in my intensive meditation's with Bryan, that at the beginning of the week, I had been feeling much better, happier and more content than at the end of the school week.

The closest word that relates to this idea is called Punya. In ancient Buddhist texts this is called earning merit and refers to the accumulation of good karma as the result of religious works, good actions or good speech.

The difference is that meditation is not a physical action and the merit earned is through your consciousness and helps to contribute to a person's spiritual growth towards spiritual liberation. The accumulation of meditative merit is what I call, adding to your spiritual bank account. But this specific type of merit cannot be found in Buddhism. It is just something I noticed myself in my practice.

CHAPTER IX

HOOLIGANS

On June 10th, 1994, the day after the last day of high school, I packed my Dodge Ram van and went downstairs with my bags packed. As I told my father I was leaving for the summer, my heart began to race. I expected him to put up a fight. With a very stern expression, he stood in front of the door and said I couldn't go on this trip. He didn't explain. I guessed that it was because he wanted me to go to college, but I wasn't sure.

Fuming, he said, "If you leave, you can't come back."

Emotion had gotten the better of him. He could have made his concern for me more clearly if he had said something like, "As your father, I'm worried you're making the wrong choice for your future. I did the same thing when I was young, and I don't want you to make that same mistake."

I could tell he was thinking this, even though he didn't say it. My heart began to calm. I looked at him silently for a few moments, then nodded, "Okay," and walked out the door.

I drove from San Fernando Valley down to Malibu, feeling free—free from high school, free from my father, free to pursue my ideals. Along the way, I would pick up my two friends, Jeff Grimm and Sean Leahman. We were going to miss the high school's graduation ceremony the next day.

I parked in Sean's driveway and walked into his house in Malibu. At this time, he didn't have a car, because he had crashed it in a canyon tunnel and almost dropped out of school. Jeff was also waiting for me at Sean's house. His mother was rich and had other plans for Jeff's summer. Both of my friends wanted to get away from their parents and needed a ride to this epic party in Northern California.

When I arrived, Jeff let me into the house. Sean was in a fight with his father in the next room. The man wanted to know how long Sean would be gone; Sean didn't know and was honest about it. That wasn't good enough for his dad.

We left quickly, jamming into my Dodge Ram van, driving along the coast from Malibu to Santa Cruz. I had picked up the van after my orange Volkswagen square back had died. Sean and Jeff had minimal luggage, just backpacks and jackets. I had an entire suitcase filled with all the clothes I owned.

My plan was to leave Sean and Jeff in Santa Cruz and continue north to Oregon and spend the entire summer at a meditation retreat center and finally meet my Guru, Sant Thakar Singh.

I pulled onto the 101 freeway and drove up past Santa Barbara and the world stretched out before us like a long, winding river, and for a moment, the possibilities were endless. We were on a summer pilgrimage, a last hurrah before college, and I had grand visions of finding enlightenment that up until this point I had kept a secret from my friends. This was to be our last summer before Jeff and I headed off to college.

We made it to San Luis Obispo. That first day was filled with a sense of excitement, music, and genuine freedom that comes when you travel and we all felt it. Over the open road, we truly felt free. We camped under the stars, told stories around our little fire, and made our own rules as we went along.

But as the night dragged on, cracks began to appear in the façade of our brotherhood. Sean's desire for recklessness was apparent like a wildfire devouring everything in its path. He brought out some drugs. It seemed like he wanted to drown out the silence of his own thoughts, messing himself up with chaotic diversions, like a psychedelic trip that would have lingering consequences.

I declined. And as I watched Jeff and Sean trip out under the stars. I went to bed early, much to the disapproval of Sean. Sean and Jeff lost themselves to the night. I, on the other hand, had embarked on this journey in search of something greater. I yearned to connect with the divine, to understand the meaning of life, and to find purpose.

As we continued to drive up the coastline the next day, Jeff asked what I would be doing after I continued up north, and told them I was going to meditate on an Oregon retreat center. Both Sean and Jeff's initial reaction was confusion.

"Why?"

Sean had a devilish grin, his eyes gleaming with the promise of wild nights and debauchery, while Jeff, the steady and more reliable one, just offered a reassuring nod.

"Why not party, smoke weed, and chase women?"

"I'm thinking meditation might solve my problems," I said.

"What problems, dude?" Sean asked in disbelief.

Sean mocked my quest for spirituality, calling it a futile pursuit. "Greg, you're wasting your time man," he scoffed, lighting up a joint. "Life's too short to be so damn serious. You got to lighten up and enjoy the ride man."

Maybe it was the long drive ahead or the ocean visible from the road, but for some reason, I was in a place to tell them what happened at Disneyland with Chris and Ryan — how I smoked weed and had a bad trip, and how the effects of that trip never quite seemed to leave me. However, since that time, for the last two years, I had suffered from guilt and depression, how I hated myself, and how after that experience, I was different, changed, with a full-blown self-conscious inferiority complex. I told them how my therapist had said this to me, how he even said he couldn't help me, and how until now I didn't know how to fix this.

"So," I said, "for me, meditation is the only answer."

"All summer?" asked Sean in disbelief. "The entire fucking time?"

"Yup."

Sean and Jeff looked at each other. They had learned the same meditation techniques I had and practiced themselves. It was possible for them to do the same thing I was planning to do, but they had an entirely different summer planned.

"That sounds interesting but," Jeff admitted.

"But stupid. That's too hardcore Greg," Sean interrupted. I began to feel like Sean was being a dick. There was a silent resentment growing towards him that I didn't know how to express.

Jeff, being more of a loyal friend, stood by my side. He could relate to the turmoil I'd been through and knew that my journey was important. He thought I was cool, with my Indian classical music, long hair and trippy style. There was no one else like me so he also tried to meditate with me when we stopped to take a piss break. And between Sean's desire for chaos and my search for meaning, Jeff found a particular sort of Zen balance. He melded perfectly between both of us, but the rift with Sean grew wider with every passing mile.

"What's your plan?" I asked Jeff.

"Actually, I plan to go to college in Santa Cruz so I told my mom I was gonna check it out. And since we're going there anyway, it's gonna work out perfectly. I'll be looking at living at a Buddhist temple."

"You guys are both too far out man," Sean said smoking another joint.

"Sounds cool," I said. "What type of Buddhism?"

"Soto Zen," Jeff nodded.

The farther we were from home, though, and the closer we got to Santa Cruz, Sean spoke up about his own experiences with meditation—how he had seen, with his eyes closed, that light which had blinded him for three hours.

"How is that even possible?" Jeff said, skeptically. "I mean, it's not. It's not humanly possible to be blinded by spiritual light coming out of your third eye."

"No," I said. "I had a similar experience like that. I wasn't blinded, but, once, when I had, like, one hundred present single-minded concentration, I saw a blinding light."

"I wouldn't mind seeing it," said Jeff, "What if you could see it on LSD?"

We all laughed.

As we reached the halfway point around noon, on another one of our crazy ass long breaks, the tension grew. Sean and I had an argument outside a liquor store in a dirt parking lot. Words were exchanged, harsh and unforgiving, like the unforgiving heat. Jeff, always the peacemaker, finally had enough. He sided with me, and Sean stormed off. The dust kicked up under his feet and looked dramatic, like something out of a movie. It annoyed me that everything looked like it was in a movie. I wanted to forget about Hollywood for the time being.

As I drove, I talked about my studies of numerous books about past lives, near death, and out-of-body experi-

ences, and how in all these books there was an Astral
Plane, and even in that world, there were higher levels of
reality that could be reached. I gave them a short history
about Yogananda and how his teacher came back to life
after he died in a resurrected, physical body, like Jesus.
How Yogananda was able to ask questions that revealed
his teacher had been at the top of the Astral Plane and
helped people who had died and were now living on a
higher other plane.

"It's my theory," I said, "that Yogananda's teacher was
able to do all this, because he practiced meditation his entire life. That's why he was able to help other people ascend
into this higher dimension. And there are more realms beyond that one, even purer realms that we can actually
reach. If you meditate hard enough, you can get to these
higher dimensions."

Sean and Jeff stared at me like I was crazy.

"So, that's what you're going to do this summer?" Jeff
said. "I think that's cool."

"You're too focused on achieving something." Sean
asked. "Just enjoy. Just live! Whatever man. Why waste
your life like that?"

I didn't respond. I was just glad we were talking again. I
didn't think it was that type of question that was meant to
be answered, but more of him voicing his own frustration
with the conflict of values. So I just stopped talking for the
rest of the drive.

That night, as Jeff and I sat around the fire, we found
solace in looking at the stars in the silence. The stars
seemed to twinkle with a knowing wisdom. I realized then
that the road had taught me something valuable. It had
shown me that life was in balance like Jeff balancing between two friends at odds, there was this delicate dance
between the wild and the serene, the spiritual and the sen-
sual.

The next morning, we found Sean waiting for us at the car, and for the rest of our journey, we found a new equilibrium.

Sean came to me privately, a hint of that familiar devilish glint in his eyes. "Greg," he said, "you've got to come with me to the Rainbow Gathering next week. Just take a break for a week and come. It's going to be an experience like no other. The ultimate spiritual journey, man."

I didn't want to say no so I just responded, "We'll see."

"Dude, you got two months bro, just come. I want you to come," Sean persisted.

It was a touching speech, an act of reconciliation on his part, which I appreciated. But I shook my head, my commitment to my own spiritual quest unshaken. "I appreciate the invitation, I do brother, but my path is different, and I need to continue my search in my own way."

"You saying you're better than me?" It was more of an accusation than a question.

"I just got a summer mission. I can't deviate. Sorry bro."

Sean's disappointment was palpable, and for a moment, I could see the frustration in his eyes. He wanted me to be a part of his adventure, to share in the excitement of the unknown. But I couldn't compromise my own journey for the sake of his desires.

Before Sean walked away, he had to have the last word. "Your guru obsession is weird bro."

I didn't respond. I felt the nature of our relationship could never be the same after this moment. I remained silent until we arrived in Santa Cruz. We finally got off the freeway and headed into town.

I think Jeff, Sean, and I were going about 90 down a 45-mile an hour road. The windows were rolled all the way down and Sean was yelling at no one in particular, or at everyone — wild coyotes about to feast. It was my last night before my spiritual servitude and I felt the thirst and the fear behind what I might do. In less than two days from now, I would sorely miss opportunities like tonight.

We drove over a bridge down Soquel Avenue into downtown Santa Cruz. The night had begun. The street lamps were piss drunk yellow and we were howling again. We pulled up outside of a large community center warehouse. Music bumped out of the back fenced-in patio. I looked over to the front entrance and saw a large group of people paying to get into the party. I didn't want to know how much tickets were.

I parked and turned off my van. Sean was gathering his things not sure if he'd see me again tomorrow, so I opened a bottle of water and emptied it.

"I got some magic mushrooms," Jeff said. "You interested?"

He displayed a zip lock bag and looked at me. I looked at Sean, but he was busy rifling through his backpack. It seemed Jeff was acting on his own here.

"Nah, man," I said, "I'm good."

Jeff shrugged and popped a couple of caps.

A heavy silence hung in the air. I knew I needed to quit doing drugs. If I was going to become a sane person, I needed to control myself. In front of us, a white Corvette made a U-turn, probably looking for a parking space. Its headlights pin wheeled across our faces as Jeff buried the zip lock bag back in his pocket.

"How we getting in?" I asked.

"Don't know," Jeff said, looking out the window. He was a little let down that I hadn't taken mushrooms with him. "My friends are already inside."

"Let's party!" Sean said, with a dramatic flourish, hopping out the back door of my van onto the damp grass.

I locked my van and Sean directed Jeff and me to the back fence of the patio where no one was standing. The wind was blowing. It felt risky, but we were young. Two minutes later, we slipped through the opening in the fence and were sandwiched between a row of women wearing translucent wraps that I guess passed for mini-skirts. Anyway, we weren't complaining. Sean looked at the women, and then he looked back at me with a huge shit-eating grin. Jeff was also smiling ear-to-ear.

One of the blondes turned and looked at me. "Oh," she said in surprise.

I smiled knowingly. Everything was cool. Sean fearlessly started a conversation. Jeff was equally as interested. I was more interested in the electric dance music that bumped hard on the other side of the pool where a large group had gathered. As I got closer, the bass was thumping, the crowd was electric, and I felt the music coursing through my veins. People were moving rhythmically, almost in slow motion. At every party, I knew where there would be a space for me on the dance floor. I walked over to one of the massive speakers and claimed my territory. No one ever danced by the speakers because they were always so loud. I didn't feel self-conscious so I danced alone, and I danced for an hour.

Out of the corner of my eye, I couldn't help but notice her - a gothic girl with raven-black hair and eyes that pierced through the haze of the party. She was dancing like she was possessed by the rhythm, and something about her drew me in like a moth to a flame. As I watched her; she twisted her hips and spun them around in a way I'd never seen anyone dance before. I loved it. I hesitated a moment. I could feel my pulse quicken. "Don't think," I said to myself and began moving my feet in her direction. I weaved in and out of sweaty dancers. People holding drinks looked at me. The closer I got, the harder my heart pounded. When I finally reached her, I didn't waste any time. I grabbed her hand and pulled her close, our bodies touched and began moving in perfect harmony. I leaned in close.

"I love the way you dance," I yelled. It was difficult to speak with the music blaring so loud.

"What?" She yelled back, leaning in closer to me, my lips now pressed against her ear.

"You're hot," I said.

She turned and faced me without blinking, without smiling, searching my face. She could see I liked her and she moved closer — leaning into my chest. We both moved our hips in rhythm to the music again.

On the other side of the pool, I saw Sean and Jeff for a moment before they walked away. They didn't seem to be looking for me and they didn't seem to care. I didn't really care, either. We had already discussed this, the prospect of getting lucky.

The girl leaned in closer, her lips brushing against my ear. "Marley," she whispered.

Now, I had her name: Marley. I thought she was pretty, but, honestly, she had on so much dark make-up and piercings that you couldn't tell what she really looked like. I had never seen a bull nose ring with spikes on each end and had lost count of how many earrings she wore. I just… liked watching her dance. And she seemed to like the attention.

She looked at me with a mix of curiosity and amusement, and I flashed my most charming smile. "Name's Greg," I yelled over the music.

We found a quiet spot away from the chaos of the party, where we could hear ourselves think. I got us both drinks. I couldn't help but feel a deep connection with Marley. We were both in search of something more, both straightedge.

The party began to die and the warehouse emptied.

"Let's get out of here," I smiled.

Marley and I ended up at an Oceanside parking lot. To find the beach, we trudged over a hill through tall yellow grass that needed weeding. She unlaced her Doc Martens so I kicked off my tennis shoes and we felt the cold sand between our toes as we ran towards the crashing waves. We sat along the shoreline, each staring off into the moonlit water, not sure what the future had in store; maybe both of us were just trying to hold onto a time that would soon be long forgotten. She told me she had two weeks before she shipped out to Vietnam to work as a translator.

The moonlight was blue and I could see the vulnerability behind her tough girl image. We were strangers and yet somehow that made it easier to just be ourselves.

I turned and brushed her hair away from her eyes. Maybe for this moment, we could forget all that needed forgetting by getting lost in each other. I leaned forward. Our noses touched and I smiled. Teasing her.

She pulled my lips to hers. And then, we shared secrets.

"I have a boyfriend who just broke up with me," she said, "because I wouldn't sleep with him. Do you think I'm weird?"

"If he really liked you, he'd wait," I said, softly.

"Really?" She said, doubtfully, poking her finger into the sand.

"Totally. If it was the other way around, would you have waited?"

Her face drowned in shadows, but I could make out a tear glinting from the light of a passing car as she looked back out over the water and nodded, letting those words sink in. She would have waited.

"I'll be gone for a long time," she said.

She paused, wanting to see what I might say to that. Maybe she wanted me to wait for her, but I said nothing for a long time. She pulled her knees tightly about her. When she looked up at me sideways, her eyes conveyed a groping sadness.

"Me, too," I finally said. Then I sighed. The invisible weight I held in the center of my chest was being mirrored back in my new compatriot. Her fingers encircled mine and our hands were frozen together for some moments. We shoved our cold hands deep back into our pockets and curled our toes under the sand. The waves crashed onto the shore like a slow methodical drum, guiding us into a short forgetful sleep.

She spun memories around her brain into a tangled mess. I whispered in her ear and pressed my lips against metal. She leaned her head on my shoulder and when she felt the desire, she bit my lip. When I glanced down, tears filled her eyes and throat. All I could see was a woman — lost, vulnerable, and alone.

As we turned our backs on the unrelenting ocean, drudging our cold feet through the damp granules of sand, I could hear her chains clank every step she took. I took her hand and interwove my fingers in hers.

I drove her back to the military base where she was stationed because she had a curfew. We arrived early, so we waited. It was as silent outside my van as it was inside. The unbearable sadness in her eyes caused the air to thicken. I tilted my head and studied those big black eyes, trying to hold on to something ephemeral.

With a reticent tone, she asked, "Why aren't you going to the rainbow gathering with your friends?"

"You know why."

"Yeah, but your friends clearly like to party," she said. "But you… you're different."

This was still so new. She was curious.

"I'm not like anyone else you'll ever meet." I said, grinning with mischief.

"No," she said.

Marley blinked and bit her lips. Her dark eyes looked like pools filled with ice cold water. If you were to take a swim in those eyes, you might freeze to death.

"My parents used to be hippies, like my friends," I continued. "They taught me there was more to the hippie revolution than doing drugs. And yet that's mostly what their generation left behind. I mean, I've had my own experiences with drugs. That's one reason I'm straight edge now."

She nodded.

"I'm straight edge, too," she said, "and I was raised Christian. I don't go to church, but I still want to wait until marriage and stuff."

"Don't lower yourself to some dummy's standards who doesn't even really care. Otherwise, he'd wait." I didn't mention that I was still a virgin.

"Yeah," she said. Her voice seemed far off and lined with sadness.

"My parents met at a meditation center. It made it easier for me to be open-minded."

She looked at me for a long time. I looked at her lips. She had reapplied her lip gloss. I took a bite. Her lips tasted like strawberries and bubblegum. I ran my fingers through her hair, pulling her black bangs away from her eyes, which now seemed hollow and lost. But their spark hadn't completely fizzled. There was a flickering flame. That was new.

"Can we meet tomorrow?" she asked.

I gently pressed my lips against the white skin of her forehead and could smell her perfumed hair. When she looked up into my eyes, it was as if I were looking down into a well. She didn't smile, but showed herself raw.

I heard her metal chains hit my van door as she slid out of the seat. I watched these chains hang against her slim waist, clanking and clanking away as she walked back onto base and through the rusted doors of her dormitory. The door snapped shut behind her.

I leaned my head back and smiled. We had shared something. That's what she wanted from her boyfriend, I imagined, to feel seen, heard, and respected. I also needed that. None of my high school relationships even came close to being this honest. Honesty was something for which I was developing a new appreciation.

I drove back along the beach and parked. I wasn't ready for the night to end, so I opened the side door of my van and watched the waves crash until I had to wrap a blanket around my shoulders. Darkness came and my eyes grew heavy. Underneath the comforter, my feet were toasty warm and cozy as my mind drifted.

The next day, I met up with Jeff and Sean. They thought I had left already and wondered where I had been. I told them about the girl, and they said they had become friends with a group of girls who invited us to spend the night. We hung out by the beach, walked around the city, and got some lunch.

When Jeff left to find a restroom, Sean looked at me. "Dude, we had some fun last night. When are you gonna snap out of it and have some real fun?"

I needed to address this issue. I was leaving soon and I may never see Sean again after this. I stood my ground, refusing to let his words get under my skin. My path had taken me to places I couldn't have imagined, and I wasn't about to back down. "Sean," I replied evenly, "we all find our own way in this world. This journey is mine."

It became clear the divide between Sean and me had grown too wide to bridge. Our paths had diverged, and we no longer walked the same road. We were high school friends. And now Sean was going off doing his own thing and he wasn't into what I was into like before. It was a hard truth to accept, but it was a truth nonetheless. It was time to part ways.

To my surprise, the day before I was to leave Santa Cruz, I met with the military Goth girl again. She brought me food. I was grateful and we ate in the back of my van and hung out. I didn't try to make any moves on her, although I thought she wanted something more from me, so I hugged and kissed her. We looked into each other's eyes without speaking for a long time. She knew I was leaving town the next day, and I knew she was about to leave town for two years.

That night, we went to a party. The Goth girl ended up leaving shortly after Sean, Jeff, and I had arrived, claiming she was there only to say goodbye. Her dorm was nearby, so she turned down my offer to see her home. I watched her walk into the dark. That was the last time I saw her.

After the party, Jeff and I were walking to his friend's house. We waited at a convenience store for Sean. He was thirty minutes late. Out of nowhere, Sean appeared, his footsteps echoing on the quiet street. He looked like he hadn't showered in days, wore a Mexican poncho, and smoked a cigarette clearly having a different agenda for the night. "Hey, guys," he called out, his voice slurred with a touch of intoxication. "I've got a plan. There's this girl I met at the party, and we want to spend the night on the beach. But I need your white comforter, Greg."

I couldn't believe what I was hearing. My white comforter was a prized possession, an expensive gift from my mother and I wasn't about to let it become a casualty of Sean's reckless adventure. "No way, man," I replied firmly. "I don't want to get it dirty out on the beach."

Sean rolled his eyes, clearly exasperated. "Don't be weird," he scoffed. "You're too attached to material things. It's just a damn blanket."

"Just bring the girl back to Jeff's friend's place," I suggested, my tone unwavering. "It'll be warm in there."

Sean's expression darkened, and he muttered something under his breath. He wasn't used to being denied, especially not by me.

With a sour mood, Sean turned and walked away, disappearing around the corner. Jeff and I continued on our way to his friend's house, the weight of the unspoken tension hanging in the air. It was a stark reminder that some bonds, no matter how strong they once were, could be broken beyond repair.

A bunch of UC Santa Cruz students lived at Jeff's friend's house, no adults. At dinner, some of the female housemates made and sorted out beds, and that night, I ended up in bed with two hippie girls I'd never met before. They seemed cool. We turned off the lights and everyone went to bed. I fell asleep instantly and had a lucid dream. I reminded myself that I was dreaming. As I stood there in the dream, now fully aware I was in a dream, I heard a voice.

"If you don't make a move on these girls now," the voice said, "You'll never make a move."

I was still very much asleep, inside the darkness behind my closed eyes, somehow standing in this dark, surrounded by a hazy smoke.

"Okay," I said, in the dream. "Make the move."

This was the first time a voice suggested something and I listened. To whom did this voice belong? Why did I agree? Is one even responsible for things one agrees to do in a dream? How would that even be fair?

When I opened my eyes, my hands were already in motion without my knowledge, touching a girl's arm and breast. However, she didn't object. She began touching me, and then the other girl joined in, too. The three of us began kissing on this large King-sized mattress. I was nervous, but I had already made a move; I wasn't sure how to stop. The girls were responding. Things were just happening naturally. At some point, during all this, I fell asleep again, too afraid to take things further.

The next day—the girls and I, Jeff and Sean—we all hung out at the beach. I needed to head out, but my friends had smoked weed and I was too tired to drive. I acted awkwardly around the girls I had slept with in bed. Of course, I didn't want to act like a weirdo, but I was so nervous, I couldn't help it.

One of the other girls at the house told me she liked me.

I told her I was leaving. She looked disappointed.

CHAPTER X

UAP

At dusk I left my high school friends behind, determined to reach Oregon. I had never traveled through Northern California, however, and didn't exactly know where I was going. By chance, a guy at the party offered me gas money for a ride home. He showed me the way out of Santa Cruz on the way to my destination, as I was so happy to believe. We conversed casually until I talked about meditation. He was very curious to know when I had started.

"I got initiated by my father's Guru at sixteen," I said, "and had some cool experiences. I saw a worm hole once with closed my eyes."

"That's impossible," he frowned and looked puzzled. "Were you high?"

"Nah, I saw a circular geometric shape with intricate details," I explained. "It looked like a mandala which represents the universe in Hindu and Buddhist symbolism. In a dream, a mandala is supposed to mean that the dreamer is searching for completeness and self-unity."

"Is that what you were doing? Dreaming?"

"No, it's not dreaming exactly," I said. "It was more like... a vision? I mean lucid dreams happen in the middle of the night while you're sleeping. This happened in the night when I sat up cross legged to meditate. I closed my eyes and in the darkness, I actually saw a mandala and got sucked up into it."

"What do you mean?"

"I don't really have an interpretation for it. It just happened and I went with it."

I drove him over the coastal hills east of Santa Cruz County, to a small town in the central valley off the 5 freeway. Before getting out of the car he handed me enough cash to fill the tank, with pocket change to spare. He also gave me sleeping pills after I told him I would have to pass out in my car that night. He said offhand that the pills were the "illegal kind." I wondered what that meant.

Alone for the first time since leaving home, I pulled out my large Triple AAA foldout map and studied it to find the best route north. I needed to take the 580 toward San Francisco in order get on state Route 1 and travel the along beautiful coastline north of the city. The 5 was boring and there was nothing to see. I realized that I had gone out of my way to drop this guy off. Little did I know that this detour would prove to be stranger than fiction. I was only certain that nothing is certain.

I continued to drive up the 5, looking out at the dark landscape that stretched endlessly in every direction. The terrain seemed barren, arid, and unforgiving, with nothing to look at but what seemed like an endless expanse of darkness, shrubs, and car headlights passing in the opposite direction. The monotonous scenery offered no distractions at all. It felt like my brain dripped thoughts slowly one at a time, like an annoying leaky faucet. A tedious boredom filled the gaps between thoughts.

Feeling like I'd left my earthly home, traveling through outer space, I reminisced on a day when Jeff, Sean, and I lay on the beach in Malibu, basking in the warmth of the sun after surfing. I could almost taste the salt water lingering on my lips. That brought a smile to my face. But the smile faded quickly as I thought about what Sean and I had recently discussed. It seemed like a chapter in our friendship had closed. I didn't know if I'd ever see him again. Then I was taken over again by sentimental dreaming about surfing and the waves.

On the road to a new summer adventure in meditation, I reminisced on last summer's visit to the Monroe Institute back east. I'll never forget how elated and fully energized I felt walking through the airport after going through the workshops and the breakthrough experiences induced by binaural sound therapy. I recalled how excited I got relating that experience to Sean.

Then I wondered why I had even bothered to talk to Sean about my out of body experiences at the Monroe Institute. Maybe I thought he'd find it cool, but I didn't really care what he thought. I considered that how we talked about this to each other, talking as high school friends, was like we never would again.

I thought back on when my mother gave me Robert Monroe's book, after I became both interested and disturbed upon first hearing about her out of body experiences when I was twelve years old. I actually read through it and began to feel some relief from the confusion. I also discovered the call to a higher meaning in my life. It was like I found a piece of a very large puzzle, giving me a taste of a very deep peace of mind that, as I looked back, remains perpetually fleeting and elusive. I smiled inside myself in awe at how even as a child I had the strong motivation to find the answer to the age old mystery of death.

Where do we go when we die, I asked myself, keeping the van between the lines on the freeway, flashing hash marks keeping the beat of passing moments of time and space on the way to the unknown destination. Do we simply cease to exist like so many people believe, or is there something more? This existential dread only intensified the more I learned. I read about dead people whose souls were trapped in the astral plane because they didn't know they were dead, unable to let go of their previous life in the body, or about demons and aliens stuck there as well. I began to conceive how mythic faeries, gnomes and goblins actually inhabit strange belief zones where people get trapped by their own false ideas and illusions of the imagination that become prisons of their own making.

I remembered how I read various books, but it wasn't until I stumbled upon the writings of Yogananda that I found a glimmer of hope, which lead me on my current journey north.

But Robert Monroe's journey into the realm of out-of-body experiences first captivated me and eventually induced me to visit the Monroe Center. His book "Journeys Out of the Body," offered a tantalizing glimpse into the possibility of exploring the mysteries of existence beyond the physical realm. But Yogananda's book took it to a whole different level. Monroe's firsthand accounts of leaving his body and embarking on adventures in the astral plane were nothing short of fascinating. But Sri Yukteswar's confirmation of a land above the astral plane where you could live and exist reminded me of a place I had been and to which I wanted to return, my personal Shangri-La.

Inspired by both Monroe's experiences and Yogananda's discipline, I delved headfirst into the world of astral projection and meditation. What shocked me most were the similarities between both practices. After reading every book I could find on the subject, learning about meditation, lucid dreaming, and various practices designed to separate the consciousness from the physical body. I was determined to uncover the practical truth and have some experiences for myself. The fact that we will die is proof enough that this isn't our real home.

I began to practice meditation with my father's guru, learning to still my mind and expand my consciousness. But I had begun to get bored with Prem Rawat's meditation practice. I kept reading all the books I could about life after death and wasn't satisfied. I practiced out of body techniques on my own before making it to the Monroe Institute. At last, I found Paul Twitchell's *The Tiger's Fang*. Now I was going to put all of what I had learned together. That's when I started to look at other meditation teachers, much to my father's dismay. It had intensified our long-standing conflicted relationship, and ultimately caused him to tell me not to return home if I went to the Ashram up north to meditate. By this time, though, I was eighteen, and he didn't have any control over what I could do.

After I meditated with Bryan, I started slowly but surely to experience moments of profound clarity and a sense of detachment from my physical self. I had seen glimpses of a reality beyond this one. I had several out of body experiences. And these glimpses into altered states were both exhilarating and terrifying. I had come face to face with a possible demon, a creeper that I thought might have clung onto me when playing the Ouija board as a kid. My childhood friend had acted especially devilish when he played the Ouija board. I suspected that he attracted the dark force that attached itself to me.

Was I imaging things? I felt like I was on the brink of something extraordinary yet nightmarish. The fear lingered. I remembered how my friends laughed when I told about my fear of aliens. I was afraid of the dark because I thought they might come and abduct me at night. It was irrational. I also had a strange fear of needles. I smelled strange things that no one else noticed. Were all these emotions, fears and experiences connected?

All of these kinds of thoughts recapping my life and spiritual quest kept rolling out to the sound of the tires whining over the pavement, churning up over the warm engine humming right below me. I wondered if it was important that my grandfather was an F.B.I. agent, whose wife also had out of body experiences, like my mother, and now me? My other grandfather was a military man and so was my father. Did these facts about my family back-ground link me to something sinister that was beyond my understanding or control? Maybe. In youth it's so clear to see or imagine.

Lucid dreaming became another obsession. I kept a journal by my bedside, recording every dream I could re-member. Over time, I gained the ability to recognize when I was in a dream and take control of its narrative. Once a group of aliens came to me in such a dream. Freaked out, I punched one of them in the head. Then I realized I was sleeping, and seemed to roll out of my body. In a fog I floated above my sleeping form but couldn't see it, I reached down and touched my bed with my hands. The fabric felt real. I forgot that I was having an out of body experience. I forgot about the aliens in my room. I thought I was awake until I pushed down hard on the bed and my hands went right through it. I repeated this process several times trying to figure out what was actually happening. Eventually I woke up with the full realization of all this happening in an out of body experience.

After the 5 freeway met the 580, I headed west toward the San Francisco Bay. It was getting late when I passed several hills with quite a number of tall wind turbines. It was after nine p.m. by the time I crested the top of another lonely hill, catching my first glimpse of Bay Area lights, before heading down the long grade into Castro Valley. Being sure not to take a wrong turn, I took out my big map again, and while driving flipped it out to unfold it. I lay it out in front of me on the steering wheel, gripping the wheel over the paper.

When I looked up from the map, that's when I saw it.

At first, I thought I was seeing a large blimp or something like that. The thing was flying north, crossing the 580 at the east side of Castro Valley, heading toward the city.

I looked again. It was much too large to be a blimp. Looking at the object gave me a headache. It was difficult to keep my eyes on it, partly because I was driving, but also because the bizarre distraction agitated me.

I had to look again. The voice in my head repeated – it's a blimp.

The flying object was silver and appeared to be metallic. *What was this thing?* My mind kept saying blimp, but I couldn't see a cockpit. It was far too big to be a blimp. It moved silently and flew quite low, maybe only two hundred feet above the road.

The craft moved at a slow pace, almost hovering over the road. I had another opportunity to focus. I gathered my concentration on this flying craft. What I saw amazed me. The entire thing was covered with a circuit board-like schematic that appeared to be a silver-like metal. Was this some kind of UAP, Unidentified Aerial phenomenon? I needed to get off the freeway and find a place to collect my thoughts. Most UAP's are like small sports cars. This was the mother of all ships. It was as big as a cruise liner.

I took the E. Castro Valley Blvd. exit and made a right, then another right into a strip mall next to the 580 freeway. I pulled into the parking lot near Safeway and stopped. For a moment, I looked over my map and figured out which freeway I needed to take to go into San Francisco. I reversed out of my parking spot, but as quickly as I started, I stopped again. The UAP hadn't been in my imagination. There it was again, slowly, very slowly, flying above the parking lot.

Aside from my car, the entire lot was empty, except for three vehicles parked on the far side the strip mall in front of a Petco. The UAP was passing directly over the three cars, when one car jerked forward and drove quickly and strangely, following all of the signs even though no one else was in the lanes. The car could have easily just drove across all the empty parking spaces. I also noticed the car making strange jerky moves. It didn't look normal. I looked out my window and up into the air again, the large silver UAP slowly maneuvered over the parking lot. The second car pulled out of its space, speeding quickly and following the first car. What was strange was that both cars drove in a weird jerky motion and they both followed the road signs even though they didn't have to in the empty lot. It was a strange sight, reminding me of insects walking in unison.

I drove across the lot too, and now the third car was moving. It also drove the same way, jerky and fast, making sharp turns, following all the rules of the road. Heading for an exit, I pulled up behind the second car, and the third car pulled up behind me. My first instinct was to look in my rearview mirror at the car behind me to see the driver. I became terrified, though, that I was surrounded by aliens who had beamed down somehow from that UAP. I couldn't force myself to look in the rearview mirror. I just looked down at my lap and waited for the light to change, that's how scared I was. The fear put a metallic taste in my mouth and my eyes were glued to my knees. The light changed green. I took a deep breath as the cars ahead of me pulled out of the lot. I turned in the direction of the freeway, and kept driving. When I looked at the sky again, the UAP was gone. I hit the gas and caught up with one of the cars. I could see that the guy driving the car was a tall blond man but I couldn't see his face. I studied the license plate number. It appeared to be some sort of code. I looked around for a pen but couldn't find one and the car was gone.

I continued driving north, past San Francisco, heading to the coast. I was left feeling unsettled. I found myself looking into the rearview mirror more than normal. While

I had many strange UAP experiences during lucid dreaming, I wasn't sure what to think about the UAP I had just seen. How did that even happen? Had the Monroe Institute somehow made me more prone to randomly encounter UFO's, or even see them when others may not? The more I thought about it the more I began to remember some dreams I had. I had a ton of dreams where I saw not just one, but lots of UFO ships flying around. As I drove late into the night, I couldn't shake that strange feeling that the UFO operators knew I was there, watching them. It was as if they had wanted me to see it. But why? I mean what were the chances that I would see the same UAP twice in one night? Both times I saw it, I had a perfect very close up view as the UAP was flying so close to the ground. I shuddered thinking about it.

I looked up into the night sky and wondered if I'd ever see another UAP again. All I saw was darkness and a few stars scattered across the night sky.

After witnessing the UAP, my unsettled mind clung to an unshakable feeling. The haunting image of that large egg shaped craft lingered and made me nervous. I drove another two hours, the winding road carving across Berkeley, over the San Francisco Bay and up the coast, until I reached the eerie and lesser-known town of Guerneville in Sonoma County, nestled along the foreboding Russian River.

As I drove along the lonely road, I distracted myself by thinking of alien movies. Then I had movie idea of my own, a concept unlike any alien film I'd ever seen. It wasn't about malevolent extraterrestrials descending upon Earth to conquer or destroy, but rather, about aliens who interbred with our species, seeking a rebirth in human form, to inhabit our world. The aliens follow an intergalactic law that prohibits them from making themselves known or inflicting any harm on the natural habitat.

The heart of the movie revolves around a humanoid woman who managed to escape the alien society threatening to clone her. She flees across the galaxy, pursued by a motley crew of alien bounty hunters. She crash-lands and finds herself stuck on Earth. After hiding out in a barn and sleeping with the horses, she befriends a retired businessman who had become a farmer in upstate New York. Their friendship quickly becomes the romantic core of the story.

However, the idyllic romance is disrupted when the bounty hunter's ship touches down in the farmer's backyard. A confrontation unfolds between the farmer and one of the alien bounty hunters. In the heat of the moment, our hero unintentionally shoots and kills one of the aliens, setting off a car chase between an old Mustang and a UFO.

The accidental shooting breaks interstellar law, and the farmer who was apprehended and transported back to the aliens' home planet, finds himself on trial halfway across the galaxy, facing an unfamiliar legal system, where he is sentenced to life inside a holographic universe. The ensuing drama happens after he escapes and falls thousands of feet into a trash pile to his death. The woman collects his body, and brings him by rebuilding him with mechanical body, which can be programmed thus causing the farmer to forget who he really is. As the farmer begins to remember the woman he is in love with, he discovers that she has been cloned, and her clone bodies are being sold in the sex trade industry in order to destroy her reputation. He struggles to find the real woman he loves and eventually joins in her revolution against the prevailing corrupt technocratic imperial government.

The concept was just an idea, but I couldn't shake my UAP encounter so this was a fun way to distract myself and pass the time while driving. The story had the potential to explore questions about identity, alien intelligence, and instead of having aliens invade earth, a human could go to their planet and learn to interact with them according to their intergalactic laws.

It was late when I pulled into town and I noticed all the stores were closed. I looked for a place to park. It was very quiet and no one was around.

The redwood forest that surrounded the town was a place of ancient beauty but at night it felt more like a horror film. The gigantic trees whispered forgotten truths about our ancient ancestors. It its early American heyday Guerneville was a logging community when redwoods were harvested for premium lumber in the late 1800's. Rumor had it that the grove was a now haven for old "dead head" hippies, a place to seek solace apart from materialist society. I stumbled upon this deadbeat town because it was on the way to the ocean, like the river passing through it.

I flipped my van around and parked my car alongside a desolate road near the entrance to Armstrong Redwood Park, where towering giants loomed like ancient Native American sentinels, with branches growing into the stars. The bleak darkness outside my windows pressed in like a malevolent serial killer, and I knew I needed to sleep soon to dispel the haunting thoughts that plagued me. I couldn't stop thinking that I too would surely be abducted tonight. My brain still had too much adrenaline.

As I looked into the back of my van, trash piles had begun to collect, the bed wasn't made, everything was scattered, a pile of dirty clothes, tennis shoes, backpacks, and bits of food were laying in no semblance of order. I pushed everything off my bed next to the van's side door and made sure all the doors were locked. I'd clean up the mess later, I thought. I just wanted to close my eyes. I took one last look out the back window. I drew the curtains closed dividing the front and back seat.

I reached for the sleeping pills, a dubious remedy I had procured from the stranger I dropped off in the valley. After swallowing the bitter pills, I had a lingering lump in my throat, and felt like an idiot for trusting someone I didn't even know. But sleep came swiftly, shrouding me in a heavy, disquieting haze.

Sometime in the dead of night, I awoke alarmed, my heart pounding, and a profound sense of uneasiness enveloped me in a suffocating claustrophobia. My muscles refused to respond to my desperate commands. My eyelids, laden with an unspeakable weight, remained sealed, imprisoning me in utter darkness.

I realized with a sickening jolt that these illegal sleeping pills had rendered me paralyzed. Powerless, I was trapped in a nightmarish limbo, awake but unable to escape the darkness that pressed in on all sides. But my hearing worked just fine. I could sense everything going on inside the van and outside the van. I tried to relax because I knew I was in no immediate danger.

This was medicated paralysis. I sensed an ominous presence, a specter lurking just beyond the limits of my perception, its presence malevolent and suffocating and only existed in my imagination, but that presence seemed to be there. The night also seemed to stretch into eternity, and I lay dead, frozen and helpless, tormented by my own dark fantasies.

It was in that dark abyss that I was held captive. I realized that the mysteries of the universe were not only vast but also filled with terror. The unknown was not only a realm of wonder but a void of nightmares, a place where the line between reality and the horrific blurred into a nightmarish tapestry of fear. And one day I would need to overcome that fear, but for now my only job was to try to fall back to sleep, and soon sleep returned.

The next morning I woke up feeling refreshed. I looked out the window and saw beautiful redwoods. I took a walk among the ancient trees. Before continuing my way up the coast, I jumped into a hotel swimming pool. No one seemed to notice or care that I wasn't actually a guest. Having no towel, I used my old shirt to dry off.

I got back on the road and began thinking about a time before I moved to California, when my mother's second husband—my step-father, Rick Halpern, now divorced from her—told me he had actually met an alien when he went to the Monroe Institute. Rick said he and the alien sat together on a rock in an open field and had a conversation. The alien was green but he didn't mention what they talked about because he couldn't remember. I asked him several more questions, curious about his story. Was it actually possible to meet and talk to an alien in the out of body state? Rick then gave me Whitley Strieber's book, *Communion*, about alien abductions. After reading that book, I had been left terrified. Later, I went with a friend to see the movie adaptation of Strieber's book, which starred Christopher Walken. Ever since then, I was freaked out by even the idea of aliens and couldn't fall asleep without pulling the covers over my face.

What I saw that night in Castro Valley, though, was real — something clearly in the physical world and something connected to our society.

I was drifting further and further away from what we think of as the real world, and opening up to a strange ethereal dimension which I didn't fully understand, a world where I didn't know the rules or recognize the dangers. Still in my youth, was I really prepared to embark on this journey to the far shore, across this ocean of Maya?

As I drove, I thought back over a past experience of seeing the inner mandala during meditation; had it opened up a gateway into another dimension?

CHAPTER XI

THE ASHRAM

I drove my Dodge Ram van north, making my way along the 5 freeway, which took me into the evergreen mountains of Oregon. The outside air was brisk as I crested a ridge, below a mountain peak was covered in snow. Once I dropped down into a valley, I came upon the small town of Ashland, off to the left of the freeway.

At first glance, I imagined it might be filled with redneck country folk. But after I stopped in the town and got something to eat, I realized Ashland was one of the coolest little towns I'd ever seen. It is the home of a great theater community and a college.

Should I apologize for being judgmental? I was young and naïve and grew up in cities, Miami and L.A. for my entire life until now. I liked the youthful theatrical vibe. I saw two street performers act out a scene from Tom Stoppard's play, *Rosencrantz and Guildenstern Are Dead*. A violin player and a dancer performed after the actors ran around the corner and disappeared. At the restaurant, the waitress told me about the local hot springs, in which I took a quick dip. To my surprise, everyone at the springs walked around naked.

After filling up my gas tank, I headed back onto the 5 freeway for another two hours, then exited into an even smaller town, turned west, and followed the Umpqua River, heading downstream as the water flowed out toward the Pacific Ocean. There were only a few houses scattered along the road — and then there were no houses, only the forest.

Crossing bridges and looking down at the raging river, I felt like I was truly out in the wild. I was at least an hour off of the main freeway and about an hour away from the ocean. The clouds reminded me of a Rembrandt painting, with its deep purple tones as the light broke through dark rain clouds and speckled patches of the forest.

I drove along the Umpqua River toward the incredibly small town of Umpqua, Oregon. A little over a hundred people total lived there, but this was not my destination. I kept driving farther away from civilization and had to slow down and stop because a small herd of elk was just standing in the middle of the road.

With one hand, I held my map and checked to make sure I was driving down the right road. I scanned the side of the road looking for the small, unobtrusive sign that simply read, *Manav Kendra*.

These words translate into English as "man-making center." The philosophical idea behind this name was a place to practice concentration and discipline in order to gain wisdom through deep, uninterrupted meditation. The 300 acre property, with its gardens, orchards, woods and facilities, offers plenty of work, called selfless service or "seva." Away from the distractions of the outside world, residents keep to a simple daily routine of seva and meditation sessions. Many people referred to the place as the Ashram, because it was just easier to say, and that's what people called meditation centers in India. The group adopted a lot of Indian terminology and phrases.

Sant Thakar Singh, who was still in India, founded this particular ashram; he usually visited the center once every year or two at the end of summer. A Guru from northern India, he dressed in traditional Sikh clothing—all white, and wore a white turban on his head. He had a long white beard, which made him appear saintly. He was a modest, married older man who projected an air of dignified spiritual calm.

My emotions jumped when I finally spotted the obscure sign. Finally, I had made it! I pulled the van to a stop on rocky dusty gray gravel, which kicked up quite a cloud. I looked over my notes and read the sign again, one more time it to be certain.

The gravel road headed uphill into the forest.

To my left, there was a small field of grass and the roaring river. On the other side of the river, a tall mountain had been clear-cut by a lumber company. You could smell the fir trees and dampness in the breeze.

I put my van in gear and stomped on the gas. The tires spun on the gravel as I proceeded up the dirt road that slowly climbed the mountain.

Five minutes later, I came to a gently sloping clearing. I got out and could look down on the river below. It was beautiful here. I was truly out in the wild. Was the Ashram really this far away from the city—out in the middle of no man's land?

The Ashram was designed for people to work on their spiritual development and nothing else, but there was another meditation center that had been created by a different Guru only four and a half hours northeast of this one. The community I was about to attend disliked this other center and the controversy that came out of it. Some locals were freaking out because of what had happened over there a few years earlier at Rajneeshpuram, a town populated by up to seven thousand followers of the Guru Rajneesh.

Of course, nobody wanted to see the disaster that had happened ten years earlier in Wasco County, Oregon, to happen here at Manav Kendra. The group eventually changed the name to something more American-sounding, to allay unwarranted suspicion, and members within the inner sanctum simply called it the Ashram.

However, the two groups were totally different. Rajneesh left a manager in charge who wasn't under the direct supervision of Guru Rajneesh, and the choices this manager independently made got way out of hand. Rajneesh's movement also ran into trouble with their ashram's construction permits and its growth into a small town violating various laws including the separation of church and state. Rajneesh's manager was associated with a food poisoning attack with salmonella bacteria in several restaurants, in a bizarre attempt keep people home to influence an elections, as well as an aborted assassination plot to murder a United States attorney. Clearly this manager was taking advantage of her power position and not acting under the direct guidance of her guru she single handedly ruined the reputation of all Indian style communities that were now popping up in America. American's are notoriously fearful of cults, and unfortunately what that manager had done was reaffirm people's suspicions.

The group I was about to join promoted chastity and non-violence; the Ashram had only twenty to thirty dedicated members, as compared to Rajneesh's growth to seven thousand. Although these differences were obvious, suspicions still spread throughout the Roseburg community.

I kept driving another mile up the mountain and seemed to almost reach the top, when I came upon a wood-and-wire gate where I finally discovered my Guru's meditation center. I had to get out of the van to open the gate, and then headed up to a grass-covered parking lot in front of a large dormitory building. In front of the parking lot, there was a small, cute grape vineyard that had been well-maintained. I parked my van on the grass, and I could see a number of buildings in the distance. I could also see we were surrounded by nothing more than trees and mountains for miles.

As I stepped out of my van, I felt a mysterious excitement radiating in my chest. It was as if I were an explorer about to embark on an adventure into the unknown—a new territory where I would experience things I had only read about or imagined.

Every direction I looked was beautiful. Several rolling mountains were covered with tall evergreen Douglas Fir trees, circling the curving river valley below. The air was fresh and scented. As I walked past the grape vineyard to a gate, I plucked one of the grapes and ate it—it tasted like candy.

I unlatched the gate and took a deep, relaxing breath, and listened to the birds chirping in the distance. This was a big turning point for me. Would I like it here? I guess I'd find out. I opened the gate, walked through and wandered up the hillside to the closest building.

The first time I had met the Guru was in an auditorium at California State University of Long Beach, while I was still in high school. During that week-long program, I met with John D. again, who was the one who originally told me about the Ashram. He also shared some of his own personal experiences with drugs that had motivated him to lead a more spiritual life.

"Drugs pretend to give you that spiritual vibe, but it's really a trick of the mind," he said. "The real spiritual trip is to know yourself as soul."

"What kind of drugs have you tried?" I asked.

"I tried them all, man. Drugs show you there is something more, if you're lucky. If you're unlucky, you might get toasted and confused or emotionally raw, turned out."

"I can relate."

"When I used to get high, I felt like a dripping nano wave riding the super solar cosmic sphere, man," he said, laughing at his own joke.

"I have no idea what that means."

"Dude, it's just God speaking to us through our subconscious."

"Kind of like a dream?"

"Basically, we're one with the Universe," he said. "But people think drugs are the cure to a fucked-up life, or they think they're just a ride in an amusement park."

"I get what you're saying," I said. "Drugs can't free you from yourself. They can only point the way."

"People need to be shown that profound states of consciousness are possible. But you can do it without drugs. That's why we're here, bro."

"Right on."

John D. was born in California, but his parents were Mexican immigrants. He told me that the Ashram was a meditation center far from any town or city—that it was out in the wild—quiet, peaceful, surrounded by a vast evergreen forest for hundreds of miles in every direction.

Now that I was here, the Ashram seemed more beautiful than I imagined. It was totally secluded from the kind city life that made America, *America*, from my city boy point of view. This was a part of the United States that I had never seen before. This was what it must have been like for the old settlers back in the day. But there was a metal-and-wood fence that appeared to surround the entire property, and I wondered why there needed to be a fence, since there was no one around.

I approached the closest building.

It was a large rectangular brown structure with a green roof and a wooden balcony that overlooked the river valley. I saw a set of one-lite French doors, and that's where I entered the building. Immediately, I recognized the large room with its array of tables and chairs as the dining hall. It had the smell of fresh cooked vegetables in a health-food restaurant.

Two young women sat at a table in the middle of the room. As I approached them, they looked at me. One had a beautiful, moon-like forehead with long hair; she appeared to be in her late teens. Her eyes smiled at me, and I had to look away, not wanting to give evidence of my attraction. I looked at the other woman who had twisted around in her seat to see me. She was mildly pretty with round, wire-rimmed glasses and mid-length curly hair. She had an apologetic-look on her face that I would later learn was part of her persona.

"Are you Greg?" Her hazel eyes blinked, magnified by her round glasses.

'Yeah," I said, a little surprised.

I thought only John D. and one senior administrator named Katrina knew that I was coming. I was pleased when she read my question simply from the emotion on my face.

"Oh, I work in the office," she explained, as she rose from her chair. "I'll take you to meet John. He's waiting to give you an orientation tour. This is Maria."

She indicated the attractive young woman, who looked boldly into my eyes without blinking. My heart raced for a second, and then I smiled with a well-practiced actor's smile, a smile at which I was especially good.

"Pleased to meet you, Maria," I beamed. "My name is Greg."

"I heard," she said.

Her voice was like a warm summer wind through tall, scented grass.

"My name is Christina," said the other young woman. "This is the dining hall. And, of course, the kitchen." She indicated another room in the back. "Ready?"

"Sure," I said.

I looked at Maria again and nodded to her as we walked away. She smiled at me with a radiant glow. Now that her friend wasn't looking, it seemed to me, her smile was overtly flirtatious. The smile she gave me made my heart race, but I was here to focus on meditation and not women.

Christina and I stepped out the French doors that led to the collection of buildings I had seen from the parking lot.

"Where did you park?" she asked.

"Below the orchard."

I pointed down the hill. My car was so far away that it looked like a small gray and red dot in a field of green.

"After you unload your things, you can park behind the dining hall. That's where all the guests park."

"Sure," I said, as we walked down a dirt road to a cluster of two houses and numerous trees. "Have you lived here long?"

"Almost a year," she said. "It's nice. I like it. Most people are kind and…"

Her voice trailed off, as if some other thought had interfered.

"Most?"

"There are the disciplinarians."

She gave me a side look, as if searching my face to see how I might react. I understood she needed encouragement.

"Strict?" I said, with the warm, practiced smile of an actor.

It worked. I saw the tension in her body relax.

A young Indian woman in her early twenties walked by, pulling a cart filled with vegetables. Later, I would find that this was Kompal. Her parents came from India, and she had learned the particular meditation of the ashram in India. I admired that about her for some reason.

I think at the time I secretly wished I was Indian, as if that would somehow make me more spiritual. Kompal looked at me and smiled, and I smiled back. She looked like a super nice person, and I got the feeling that everyone here was very friendly.

But Christina didn't look at Kompal; instead, she was looking at the ground as we passed her. Weirdly, I felt like she was waiting for Kompal to get outside of earshot before she spoke again.

"Some people have all kinds of concepts and rules they want everyone to follow and assume it is their place to enforce them," she said, at last. "I try to avoid them, but many of them work in administration right beside me, and I hear them talk about, you know, what must be said to this person or that person."

"What kind of rules?

"All kinds." Christina gave me another side look, and she saw the soft smile I held purposefully on my face. "No newspapers, radio, or television. But some people sneak in a newspaper or two. You have to follow the schedule and some people don't. We need you to be where you're supposed to be, do what you're supposed to do, and not everybody follows the rules. So, it would be wise to follow the rules as best as possible."

"Don't tell me they're going to hand me a list of rules?"

"Basically, it's the daily schedule," she said. "Just follow along and you'll be fine."

"It is a meditation center," I said. "Isn't its purpose to emphasize that?"

"Yes. You're right."

I sensed she had more to say, but was fearful of being scolded if caught criticizing, or perhaps it was something more disturbing. We came to a stop in front of an old, gray two-story house with white trim.

"Good talk," I said. "Perhaps we'll continue this conversation in the dining hall the next time we meet."

Christina quickly examined my face. Her eyes darted to the corners of my eyes, to the corners of my mouth, forehead, cheeks, as if she were studying a map. She then looked at my whole face, and then stared a little too strongly into my eyes. Her face turned warm, almost pretty, and she smiled with her eyes and mouth.

"Everyone likes talking with me," she said. "Because I work in the office and know all the latest news—any big plans like when Master is coming. I know what all the administrators are talking about, and who is about to get into trouble."

"Well, I'll remember that," I said, laughing. "But I hope I don't get into trouble. And if I do, I hope you'll warn me."

"Why do I get the feeling I should keep an eye on you?" Christina said, with a sly grin.

I grinned back, scratching the back of my neck, then looked up at the gray house.

"I'm guessing this is where John lives," I said, nodding toward the front door of the fifty-year-old wooden clapboard building.

"Right, a lot of people live here," she said. "Just go up the stairs--take off your shoes first, in the front hall—and call out his name. You'll find him."

She stopped speaking and then waited, as if for a cue from me about what to do next. Then she remembered something.

"I'll see you again in the dining hall. That's where everyone meets anyway."

"Well, if we all eat at the same time," I said. "I'd like it if we could eat together."

Her face brightened. "That'd be great!"

I smiled and nodded goodbye. I was worried I might have given her the wrong signal, and for some reason, worried that she might be looking for a husband. There was a moment she seemed over-flirtatious in the same way as Maria. I dismissed these thoughts as I entered the house.

In the front hall, I took off my shoes, and placed them on shelves in one of several bookcases that were filled with different types of footwear.

CHAPTER XII

THE PYSCHIC LANDSCAPE

I reached the second-floor landing, saw five closed doors lining the upstairs hallway, and called out, "John D!"

A door opened and a smiling angular face topped with a thatch of tangled black hair popped out.

"Greg!" John said, with a grin. He spoke with a mild surfer-slash-stoner accent. "A happy... a pleasure... to see you, my friend." I first met John in North Hollywood, at the house where I attended the public program for Sant Thakar Singh, the pivotal day I went on to take initiation into the meditation practice.

He bounded to me and grabbed hold of my shoulders as a friendly greeting.

"I'll take you to the dormitory," he said. "Show you around a bit, and then to the admin office for your indoctrination lecture."

"Indoctrination?" I frowned.

"Just kidding," said John, gently pushing me toward the door. "But, yeah, one of the office staff has to clue you into the philosophy here. It'll take about an hour if you keep your mouth shut. If you ask questions, it could take all day." He laughed loudly and beamed at me with a broad smile. I knew he was teasing, or was he?

Once we had our shoes on and stood outside the gray house, John asked, "Where are your things?"

"In my van in the parking lot below the orchard."

I pointed to my vehicle in the distance.

"Sweet van, bro. Let's go get your stuff."

"Can I drive it down here?"

"No, not without special permission," he said. "We can carry it. No problem."

"I was told I could park my van behind the dining hall."

"Yeah, you could do that," he said. "It's closer to carry your bags from the orchard."

We walked up the dirt road.

"Does that fence run all around the property?" I asked.

"All one hundred acres," said John. "The Ashram has another two hundred acres outside it."

"Why is a fence even necessary?"

"Ah, come on, man, what do you think, to keep you prisoner?" John smiled, joking. "No, to keep out deer. They would eat all our leafy greens down in the garden... and to keep out the mountain lions who like our sheep."

"The mountain lions eat your sheep?"

"Not as often as they used to, now that we have the fence," John said. He seemed to be pleased to be the one explaining to me the layout of the farm-retreat center. "You see that octagon house up there?"

As we walked up the road, he pointed up the hill, slightly behind us, and to our left. I turned my head and saw an old wooden building shaped like an octagon.

"Yes."

"That is the main meditation hall," he said. "Most everyone goes there to meditate every night. We listen to a videotape of Sant Thakar Singh and then meditate for at least an hour. It's called the Octagon House. For me, if I meditate more, it helps keep me stay sane. That's all good, isn't it?"

John smiled broadly. I looked at him and, for an instant, saw a flash of crazy turmoil in his large blue eyes.

"Behind us, down the road, are the storage sheds, barns, and gardens," John said, jerking his thumb over his shoulder.

I turned and looked past a cluster of two houses and surrounding trees to see dark-gray wooden structures and tilled fields with crops.

"They may assign you to work there," John said. "That's where I work. You like coffee?"

"I don't drink coffee," I said, "Anyway, I thought caffeine wasn't allowed."

"It's not—you won't find it in the kitchen, but in the work shed, I have a set-up where we have coffee every morning." He said this with a trace of pride, as if it were a significant achievement. "There is a donation jar to buy sugar and more coffee when we run out."

"So, what, this coffee set-up you got going is kind of hush hush?"

"The rule-makers don't come to the work shed and no one's gonna tell them."

"Do you know Christine?" I asked, as we proceeded to the parking lot.

"Careful what you say around her," warned John. "She works in the office, knows computers. That's where all the managers work. Not saying she would tell a secret on purpose, but if she doesn't know it's a secret, she could say something to get you into trouble."

We walked across the field and retrieved my backpack, sleeping bag, and duffle bag from my van.

"Nice wheels," John said, throwing my duffle bag over his shoulder.

"Thanks," I said. "It's a stick. They don't make too many Dodge vans with a stick shift."

"Sweet. We'll have to sneak into town one of these days and catch a movie, or go get some Indian food up in Eugene."

"They allow that?" I said, as we started walking up the hill, past the grape orchard.

"As long as no one in the office finds out, we should be fine," he said. "I got an idea. Tell them you'd like to park your car at the upper campground. That way, if you wanted to slip into town, no one would notice when you left."

"Good idea," I smiled. I felt as if I had just received some top-secret information.

"You know," John said, "I didn't think you'd come. You seemed to have too good a life in Los Angeles. But now you're here. I'm glad."

"Things change," I said. "I had a bad acid trip that fucked me up. I went straight edge. I've been using meditation as medication, but I can't seem to break out of this depression."

"That's deep, bro," he said. "I'm sorry to hear your troubles. I told you before I was doing all kinds of drugs, too."

"I remember."

John explained the layout of the property—where the administrative offices were, the dormitory, the private apartments that housed the long-time older staff members. They mostly kept to themselves, he explained, while the younger staff mostly hung out in the dorm or the dining hall, and the ones who knew about the secret coffee barn hung out there late at night.

He reminded me again not to tell anyone else about the coffee set-up. As he said the words, his face tightened. I could make out a hint of anxiety. He smiled, brushing it off.

Inside the dorm, John pulled out a white piece of paper—the daily schedule—which he casually mentioned would control my life. Everyone got up at four a.m. and there were three meals a day, served every day, at the same time. Meals were the time to hang out and chill. I'd be on a rotation to do kitchen clean-up and dishwashing. Who worked and when, down the hill in the garden, were all on the schedule.

"I saw a UFO once," John said, abruptly.

"Me, too." I looked at him, curiously. "Where? Here?"

"Yeah," he said. "There is a small cabin up the hill in the woods. It's a fifteen- minute walk, following the ridgeline. You have to go outside the gate and walk in bear country. It's a bit scary at night, so I only go during the day. No one stays there overnight because there is a rumor that it's haunted. But there's a wood stove for heat. I go there to meditate sometimes."

"You'll have to show me."

"It's right here on the map."

He pointed to a drawing of a small building pretty far away from the rest of the Ashram. There was a dotted line indicating a dirt trail that led you deep into the woods along a ridgeline that overlooked the Umpqua River valley below.

"That's interesting," I said, picking up the map and studying it.

"I meditated once out there all day and I fell asleep," John said. "It was so dark I couldn't even see my hand right in front of my face."

"Were you scared?" I asked, with a sly grin, teasing him a little.

"Hell, yeah, I was scared," he said. "Let me see *you* go there at night and forget to bring a flashlight. I really had to go to the bathroom, so I walked outside and relieved myself right off the deck. Normally, I would walk down into the grass below, but I was so scared I just unzipped my fly right there on the deck. I had no idea what the time was— maybe midnight—and as I'm taking a leak, I look up at the stars, and I see this glowing sphere, hovering stationary in the sky…"

"The Moon?"

"No, man, not the Moon," John laughed. "It was much smaller than the moon, but bigger than a star. Then it just took off at a great speed to another spot and stopped there. I watched it for a minute. Then it sped away. I think, why did it come here? Nothing else was around here for miles and miles."

"You think it knew you were there?"

"My awareness had expanded. I felt like, because of the meditation, that I could communicate with it. I got a sense it was watching me." John paused, then added, "I definitely didn't feel alone."

"Wow. What did you do then?"

"I took off running!" he said. "I ran back down the trail as fast as I could. I've never gone back to that cabin at night. But don't listen to me. I'm probably crazy!"

John began laughing and didn't stop laughing. His laughter made you want to laugh too.

"I see what you're saying. But you were probably just imagining things."

His face changed and seemed disappointed. I felt badly, as if something was wrong and I didn't know why.

"Thanks for sharing your story," I said. "I'll tell you my UFO story sometime."

"Right on," John said.

He opened one of the doors inside the dorm, which had my name written on it. There was another tag on the door with a second name—someone called Prem. John and I dropped off my gear into what would be my room. It had unfinished wooden walls, ceiling, and floor. The bed sheets looked super clean. Definitely small, it contained only bunk beds made of two-by-fours and plywood. I put my things on the lower bunk.

John led me back into the hallway and showed me the men's bathroom and the common area. It contained padded couches, padded chairs, a wooden table, chairs, and a cast-iron pot-bellied wood burning stove. There was a library with books from the Masters. The room had plenty of windows with floral curtains.

"You ready to head up to the office?

"Sure," I said, nodding.

"I'll take you to the manager's office," John said.

We left the dormitory and walked up the hill.

"Just agree to all the rules," John said, pointing his finger at me. His statement almost sounded like a threat. "If you follow the schedule, show up on time, and don't miss your dishwashing shifts, you should be fine. But if you don't follow it, you'll get in trouble."

"What kind of trouble?"

"You have to go to the office and they'll give you a warning," John said. "Do you know a girl here named Maria?"

"Yeah, we've met."

"Well, last year she got kicked out for dating one of the staff," he said. "That rule cannot be broken."

"Seems like they let her back in."

"We're not Nazis," he said.

"Isn't making coffee breaking a rule?"

"That's different. Some rules are meant to be broken. We're only human. But I don't like the office. And I don't want to get kicked out. So just say you'll follow all the rules and I will show you later which rules you don't have to follow. And remember, watch out for Christine because she works in the office."

"She seems nice," I said. "A little shy."

"Sure, she's nice," he said. "Everybody here is nice. She's kind of looking for a husband."

"How do you know that?"

"She's from Switzerland and has Green Card issues," he said. "Also, Warren is cool but he is in charge of the maintenance team and has to talk to the managers on a daily basis. So don't be too open with the managers of the people who have to report to them."

"Why not?"

"The managers take…." John paused, trying to think of the right words. "Like pride or joy in enforcing rules. You know what I'm saying? That's all they do is run around chasing after people trying to get them to follow the rules. I think it goes against the whole purpose of the meditation center, you know."

"Otherwise it would be anarchy," I said smiling.

"Right," John paused, realizing I had set him up for that one. "You'll understand later," he acknowledged my meaning. "They're just doing what the Guru told them to do, but what I'm saying, man—just be careful who you trust."

"That's a little heavy, but okay."

"Check in tomorrow with Warren about your work. You'll find him in the dining hall when everyone comes for breakfast. Ask him what you should be doing for Seva."

"I thought you said I shouldn't talk to Warren," I smirked.

"You need a job to do here man. And Warren is your guy."

We approached the front office steps.

"Look, I don't mean to be a downer," he said, "but you'll thank me later."

John left me by the front steps and walked away. So I'd have to live with other people here, enter the community and be a part of the group. I hadn't really thought about where I'd be living. The dorm seemed like a nice place to live but I'd have a roommate. Who would my roommate be?

CHAPTER XIII

INDOCTRINATION

I shut the door of the office behind me, and a man who sat at a desk facing that door looked up and smiled. He was about forty-seven years old and had thick brown hair and a bushy brown beard. He looked like a cross between a Hindu *sadhu* — an ascetic holy man — and a lumberjack.

"You must be Greg," the lumberjack sadhu said.

I looked over the lumberjack's shoulder and saw Christine at a corner desk, looking over the top of a computer screen. She was looking at me. I winked at her discretely, then looked back at the man with the beard and nodded.

"I'm Eric," the lumberjack said. "Have a seat"

Eric gestured to a chair next to his desk.

"The schedule, four a.m., wake up, go for meditation… you can read it," he said, handing me a printed sheet with the activities and times.

Next, he gave me a list of different jobs around the Ashram: meal preparation, cooking, cleaning, gardening, laundry, picking fruit, and facilities and landscape maintenance.

Eric pointed to a slim woman, about forty years old, with black wavy hair and a kind, gentle face.

"This is my wife, Erica," he said. "She is in charge of the garden crew. One of these mornings you will go with her to work in the garden."

Erica walked up and said in a thick German accent, "Hello, Greg, very nice to meet you. Welcome." Her tone was sincere. She was soft spoken with a sing-song rhythm. "So glad you are here."

"Another thing," Eric continued. "One of our young men, Patrick, had to go into town to have a vehicle repaired. He's not going to make it back in time for dinner. He was scheduled for kitchen clean-up. I was hoping that you could take his place."

"Sure."

"There's another person scheduled," he said. "I think it's Maria. We always assign two people to work on clean up duty. She'll show you what to do. Just go to the kitchen after the meal and introduce yourself. Do you know who she is?"

Eric looked at me closely.

"Nah, I don't," I lied.

Why did I lie? Was I scared of Eric? Did John influence me? There was something about him that made me want to hide the truth. I think John might be right. I could sense that the adults here had a different vibe than the younger crowd I'd met thus far. I better tread carefully.

I could see Christine's eyes pop up from behind her computer screen and look at me with stark concern. Her look suggested to me that there was something I should be concerned about, too. Had she overheard me lying about not knowing Maria?

"Eric, I was wondering if it would be okay if I parked my van at the upper campground?"

"Sure, I don't see why not. Did you see the cabin?"

"I did," I said, nodding.

"Beautiful, isn't it?" He smiled and, suddenly, I felt at ease in his presence.

"Totally," I grinned. "I can't wait to spend the day meditating up there."

Eric had me sign a number of papers, which I did without reading.

Next, I went into a private meeting room, and an older angelic-looking woman came in who I hadn't seen before. Her name was Beatrice and she wore all-white Indian-style clothing.

"Are you ready?"

"Are you going to tell me the rules?" I joked.

She laughed. Her friendly manner made me feel at ease.

"Let's begin. So, you came here to live a spiritual Godly way of life. Although we are not monks or nuns here, there are certain things we should think about."

"Okay," I said, sincerely.

"The idea is you want to have a deeper experience of meditation, right?"

"That is the idea," I said, somewhat surprised.

I thought she was going to lay down some serious rules.

"Perhaps even have a very powerful, very beautiful experience?"

"Mmm," I nodded, liking where this conversation was going.

I relaxed back into my chair and listened intently.

"In the world, it's hard to maintain a spiritual state of mind," said Beatrice. "But here, we are away from all that. That's the aim. We have a beautiful lineage of Gurus going all the way back to Guru Nanak."

You might begin to wonder what the differences are among the various designations of spiritual teachers. Indian culture contains an Acharya, who is a teacher, and a Guru, who is a realized Master. You may address a monk as Swami; the monk may be a Master or a teacher or a student.

A Guru is a Master who has followed a yogic path and realized the Truth, obtaining the state of *nirvikalpa samadhi* (which may be defined as a higher state of awareness, in which the ego and samskaras — stray thoughts in the subconscious — dissolve, and only Consciousness remains. There's no mind here as one might think of a mind — there's only bliss and infinite peace).

A Master is someone who has complete control over his mind, his breathing, and all other systems in his body. He's constantly conscious of his inner self and God. Beatrice explained that, since Guru Nanak, who lived in the 15th century, the most recent Masters include Sawan Singh, Kirpal Singh, and The Ashram's present teacher, Sant Thakar Singh. There are other examples and traditions of spiritual Masters, but we focus on the impulse of the living Master. We also benefit from the words, or spiritual discourse of all Masters in the lineage.

"We have an evening program every night, starting at seven, where we listen to an hour-long talk and then meditate for another hour or more. Some people try to meditate all night long. You don't have to do that, but you're welcome to stay in the meditation hall all night long."

"Do people really meditate here all night long?"

"A few," she said, then continued. "Sant Thakar Singh was an engineer and he was married. He used to be a Sikh, but Sikhs, like Christians, study and take inspiration from their holy book, but do not take on a spiritual teacher. Sant Thakar Singh became the Guru after Sant Kirpal Singh died. A group of confused and angry Sikh men came with swords and threatened to kill him, but Sant Thakar Singh talked to them lovingly and calmed them down. Several people had inner visions of him standing next to Sant Kirpal Singh, showing them he was the successor of Kirpal."

"I'm familiar with the stories," I said. "I've read a lot of Kirpal's books as well as Sawan Singh's books as well."

"That's good," she said. "We have a library here if you would like to check out any of their books. The Master is just the example. The idea is to realize yourself as Shabd, and connect with the Sound. You may see pictures of Sant Thakar Singh around, but that doesn't mean we are worshiping him. We just respect him as the ideal. This is a spiritual science. The message is to always connect to God within. Seek God within and find it first hand through meditation. That is always the message."

"Sounds cool," I said.

"We are spiritual scientists who are exploring through meditation. The practice becomes an important beneficial influence on your life. When you sit regularly, you will imbibe the knowledge coming through of Shabd, the inner Sound. It will clean your soul to prepare your ascent. This spiritual practice is called Shabd Yoga. Shabad and Shabd—there are alternate spellings of the Word; this is an Indian word, which means sound or music. So, we focus on the sound current and the goal is to listen to the sound and follow it back to its Source. Once your soul merges with the Source of sound, then you've reached the goal. You've probably already heard this all before."

"Yes, but the mind is forgetful," I said. "So, it's great to be reminded."

"Good," said Beatrice, pleased. "Every time I talk about this, I feel recharged. The Third Eye is the inner eye of understanding. Once you understand this knowledge, you've opened up the Third Eye. Understanding it is experiencing it. In deep states you become one with it"

I looked over at a diagram that had a drawing of an oval and several concentric circles inside it. At the heart of the page was the Earth. Each bubble was labeled.

"What is the difference between the Astral World and the Soul World?" I asked.

"Okay," she said, with a laugh. "This is a map how to get home, if you want to go home."

"Home meaning the Source – God?"

"We actually come from a world of light," she said. "It is known as the Land of Truth, and it is above the Realm of the Gods, or the Celestial Heavens, where Devas, who are divine beings, as well as Gods and Goddesses, live. I don't know how much you've studied this diagram before."

"A lot," I said.

"Okay, remember how we used to play the game called telephone?" Beatrice asked. "Where we tell someone something, and they tell the next person, and it goes down the line, and before you know it, the original message has been totally transformed?"

"It's kind of what happened to Christianity," I said. "People lost the original meaning."

"Yeah," she agreed, enthusiastically.

She could see I was paying close attention to her lecture, which inspired her to talk more in-depth.

"This happens to most religions," she said. "Different branches fight each other. Politics confuse proper understanding. They preach that God is a judgmental being to be feared, that you must behave and feel guilty for your sins. And then there is the Guru trip, making people follow instructions on empty words, pushing blind faith, and all purity is lost."

"What do you know about the subtle world, or the spirit world, where you go after you die?" I asked. I'll never forget how I learned it first from Paramahansa Yogananda, who mentioned how the divisions of reality – from the Physical to the Astral to the Causal – were each successively subtler than the last. Always curious, I wanted to hear her explanation.

"There are three worlds that have five grand divisions," Beatrice said, nodding. The first is where we are, the Physical World where we have a physical body. The next stage within and beyond all this rests in the Astral World. Our Spirit Body looks like our Physical Body there. We have glimpses of it in dreams. It is the realm of spirits and ghosts, purgatories, hells and so-called heavens. It is much vaster than the physical universe. Beyond the Astral the soul can earn entry into Causal Plane, the Celestial Heavenly World, where we take on a Godly form. After losing the Astral body, we exist within the spiritually refined Causal body until our final karma is mitigated, before entering the Maha world, where we have no body at all. Maha means great, and the souls that reach this subtle realm, have been freed from all attachments and bonds to the lower worlds. Also called the Super Causal Plane, it expands within and without, into yet more exponential vastness, a silent peaceful space where we just float as balls of divine light, where we don't think, where we just be. It's been described as a world of golden red light.

The Maha realm and the souls within it, however, still exist within the egg-shaped Universe, which is subject to Grand dissolution. At the time of the Great Destruction, the four lower worlds of God's Creation dissolve back into the source. Souls stuck there would miss out on progressing further, not reaching Sant Lok, the Fifth Plane, to be in the lap of God where the soul is said to progress through even more indescribable regions, experiencing inconceivable conditions of true being, consciousness and bliss.

"So, to make it to Sat Lok, you must break out of the egg-shaped Universe and cross the Great Void. The only way to escape the Void is to be led out by a Master Soul who has the power and knowledge to navigate that Sea of Darkness. Once the Master guides you across, *then* you enter the Realm of Truth, where you become one with God, like a drop of water merging back with the ocean. The drop and the ocean are no longer separate. It is a realm of pure light. The light there is as bright as one million Suns.

"When you look back on the worlds below, they look like a small bubble. You've escaped the realms of Maya, or illusion, that is controlled by time."

Beatrice looked at the clock on the wall. "Speaking of time, let me try to bring it back down to earth so we can get busy. To get anywhere spiritually, we must not only meditate, but maintain pure living habits. It's very important to maintain chastity. So... relationships are not allowed here."

"I noticed there are a few people here who are married," I said.

"Yes, and the manager had a son here."

"And the Master is also married. So, I assume it is allowed for people to get married?"

"Yes, that is acceptable."

"I see."

Beatrice handed me a blank notebook and pen.

"Here is a personal diary," she said. "Mark down your mistakes in lust, anger, and greed. And put down how many hours a day you meditate."

"Sounds good," I said. "Anything else I need to know?"

"We're lucky to be here," Beatrice answered. "We are trying to create Heaven here and that takes work. So, you're going to do six to eight hours of service every day. Sometimes people make fun of us and call us Love slaves because we help out for free, but we believe the work burns off our negative karmas, to help free us from rebirth into this world again. We believe that Heaven and Hell are in this world. And this place can become Heaven on Earth."

"Sounds beautiful," I said. "I've experienced Hell on Earth."

"Really? What was your experience?"

"When I was sixteen I took LSD at Disneyland. I fell into a bad trip especially after I also smoked marijuana. And it was literally the most Hellish place on Earth," I said, laughing. "It certainly wasn't the 'Happiest Place on Earth.' It was the opposite for me. I can really relate to this idea that Hell is here in this world. There is so much suffering. It's really sad."

"Yeah, all you have to do is turn on the news," Beatrice agreed. "That's why we don't have any televisions here or newspapers. In the Golden Age, we realize we are souls of the same essence of that Divine Consciousness. Our thoughts are extremely powerful. We are Pure Beings. But right now, we are in a battle between good and evil. But what is evil? It is just those five vices? What is sin?"

Beatrice's lecture seemed to be getting out-of-control, a non-stop monologue.

"In Hindi, sin means loss," she said. "So, we've just lost our soul's vitality. We all have our dark side and our beautiful side and we sometimes get lost in it. But we never become totally dark. People who are doing horrible things have just been cut off from their humanity. Deep down, no one wants to hurt another person.

"In meditation, it's beautiful to feel compassion for the world, and see the world surrounded in pure light. And the more I meditate, the more I can fill myself with unconditional love. And I can say I've had the most beautiful experience: Feeling pure love.

"Let God love you, Greg.

"The Supreme borrows a body to come down and teach us. That's why we love and respect the Master. Just like Jesus said, 'I and my Father are One,' the Master's soul has also merged back with the Supreme Soul and can therefore be an example for us. The proof is in the pudding. It's not like we're blind followers. You will see that the more you meditate. We are all very practical people. I went to India and well... I've said too much. You have to find the Source for yourself."

"Okay," I said, once she took a break. "So how do you find the source?"

"We link to the Source through meditating on the Sound. The Sound was the first manifestation of Creation. So, to become one with the One, we must meditate on the One. Yoga means union with the Soul into the Over soul, so we meditate on the Sound. We do Shabd Yoga—Sound Meditation.

"As a soul, you will actually be able to fly, but we are limited by the physical body. By listening to the Sound, you will understand where the consciousness of the Supreme is coming from. And you will be able to burn off your karmas.

"Karma is your teacher. It is coming to tell you that you can't get away with this, anymore. To free ourselves of karma, we need to burn them off by meditating on something outside of the Realm of Karma. And that's the Sound coming down from Heaven. And so, first, you realize yourself, meditating on this awareness and reflect on this. Experiment. See if it works, and check it out. That's it."

Beatrice paused. I couldn't quite believe she was finished.

"I'm glad you're here," she said.

"Thank you."

I stood and shook Beatrice's hand. "That was a great talk. I thought it was going to go a little differently, and I was pleasantly surprised. You're a good speaker."

"Oh, thank you," she said, blushing.

In moments, I was outside, walking toward the dorm.

Back at my room, I arranged my things and rolled out my sleeping bag on the lower plywood platform of the bunk bed. I was organizing my stuff when my roommate came through the door. He was tall and had wavy black hair and pale skin.

"I'm Prem," he said. "You must be Greg."

Soft-spoken with eyes that sparkled intelligence, he seemed to be my age.

Later, after dinner, I went into the kitchen and met with Maria.

"Hey, Maria," I said.

"What are you doing here?" she said, surprised.

"I guess Patrick is busy. They sent me to replace him."

"Oh, okay," she said. "Do you want to wash the dishes or dry them and put them away?"

"Well, since I don't know where anything goes, do you mind if I wash?"

"No, that's fine."

We both put on aprons and began washing dishes.

I asked Maria questions about her past. She had come to the Ashram because her father was unstable and she and her mother also had issues.

The more we talked, the more I felt attracted to her.

After we finished the dishes, she asked if I wanted to go for a walk, but I said I had a long drive getting here and that I was totally beat and needed a shower.

She seemed disappointed as I headed back to my room.

After a shower, I got dressed and headed up to the meditation hall. I arrived early; there was no one in the room. I meditated for two hours. Then everyone came in and someone started the video.

The talk was similar to the lecture I'd received. The basic message was that we have a great opportunity in this life to realize ourselves as "Soul" through meditation. Sant Thakar Singh referred to *The Bible* and several Hindu scriptures as he gave some analogies as well as morality tales.

I fell asleep during the talk because the chair I was sitting in was so comfortable. I had three pillows behind my back and head and covered myself with a thick blanket. After the hour-long lecture, it seemed like I couldn't remember any one message that the Master had talked about. But I did feel motivated to meditate. I had some experiences up to this point, and so I knew what my soul felt like, and I knew what he was saying was true. If I meditated, I could connect to my soul and potentially connect to God. Whether or not I would actually be able to know God was still up for question, but I was willing to try.

The next day, I followed a similar routine.

At breakfast time, I got some oatmeal and sat down along at a long tan dining table. There were about fifteen people in the room. Some sat alone. Others sat in groups. I saw Warren. Several people were talking to him so I waited. When there was an opening I walked up to him.

"Hey Warren," I smiled. "I'm Greg."

"I heard, welcome," he smiled back. "You're from Southern California, L.A. right?"

"Yup, a long ways off from here I guess."

"City boy, huh? Well I hope you like it up here with us country folk," He patted me on the shoulder.

"Thanks. So I heard you're the man who will help set me up with some work."

"That's right. Today we're going to do some limbing."

"Limbing?"

"Cutting the lower branches off of fir trees. Meet me down by the tool shed and we'll grab some chainsaws."

"Chainsaws?" I wondered aloud. I was a city boy about to experience the country life. I walked back into the kitchen and helped out with the dishes. I changed into something that I didn't mind getting all torn up, but I only had tennis shoes. I wandered my way down from the Dorms to the Tool shed. It was a two minute walk, passing cherry trees along the way. You could just reach up and pluck the dark red cherries. I plucked a few and spit the seeds into the grass. A few deer also ate the cherries that had fallen to the ground. Along the way I passed several people. They all introduced themselves and asked me where I came from. So the two minute walk turned into a ten minute walk.

"I'm Greg from L.A.," was my quick reply.

Warren showed up right on time. He gave me a hand-saw and he grabbed the chain saw. Another guy joined us. His name was Gabe. He had a tool belt with everything you might need working out in the woods. He had a beard and was tall but looked kind of like a Mormon. Gabe had a kind hearted smile and was a little soft spoken. The three of us headed up to the upper trail above the meditation hall and walked into the woods. My job was to cut off all the branches from the base all the way up to about six feet. I got started sawing. The work was very physical and mostly we worked quietly. But Warren and Gabe seemed to have a lot in common and talked about something I knew nothing about so I just kept quiet.

"The sun coming through the trees is real pretty," is about all I said for over an hour.

"Yeah, I know," Warren agreed.

"It's nice. I think we can drag the limbs down into a burn pile," Gabe said.

"Yeah, I think if we're gonna do a lot of this we should get some kind of a choker," Warren replied. I didn't know what a choker was. Gabe and Warren fiddled with a long metal cable that choked the bottom of the tree trunks dragging them down the hill with their truck. While I dragged the trees down into the field from off the hillside, they unloaded the trees into the large pile out in the tall grass. I couldn't believe how beautiful this place was. It was so quiet in the forest. You could hear the soft wind breeze on through. I looked up the road, which disappeared into the forest. This must be the path to the cabin John was telling me about yesterday.

"These shoe laces keep coming undone. I just bought these shoes two weeks ago," I said as bent over to tie my shoe laces for the fourth time.

Warren and Gabe looked at my shoes and laughed. They were both wearing boots and my shoes looked old now, covered in dirt and twigs. I had city boy problems.

"Maybe you guys should invest in a chipper like the one that guy used up there at the upper pond," Gabe commented looking at all the branches lying around on the ground.

"Yeah, that machine was pretty quick," Warren said.

"Did he chip up entire trees with it?" Gabe asked.

Warren looked up and pointed to a medium size evergreen tree. "He can take a tree like that and pulverize the entire thing in like five seconds."

"It's like a twenty thousand dollar machine," Gabe commented.

"Yeah, you got to put a lot of money into that stuff. He had a skid-steer, top end, and he said the engine burned up. So he's going to see if his insurance will cover it."

Gabe whistled, knowing it would burn the bank book to have a skid steer's engine burn up. I had no idea what a skid steer was.

"Yeah, it will probably cost over ten thousand to fix," Warren said. "Can you imagine how much his insurance costs? Probably twice the amount of his equipment."

"It's pretty amazing, that wood chipper. It can work so quick," Warren added.

"Alright, so is that a load?" Gabe asked as he threw another branch into the back of the GMC truck's trailer.

"Yeah, that's a load, I'll pull it out of here," Warren replied. "Will you be around later today?"

"Yeah, I should be around," Gabe said. "I was gonna say it looks like a mess."

We all looked at the hillside covered with sawed off branches.

"Right. I'm just gonna pull a couple of these limbs out of the road first."

"I'm thinking I'm gonna call it," I said feeling tired.

I said my goodbyes and walked away back to the dorm where I enjoyed a hot shower and a fresh clean set of clothes.

We got to meditate for an hour before lunch. I had to walk back up the hill to the meditation hall where I fell asleep. I didn't get in much meditation because I was so tired. I woke up feeling rested though when the lunch bell rang. The lunch bell was a loud clang that came from down the hill. The cook was smacking the metal with a long piece of wood and suddenly I felt like some school-boy, hearing a lunch bell, or one of Pavlov's dogs.

I ate lunch with John out on the patio, and then found out that I was to fill in on dishwashing to replace Maria. She had left the center. I never did sit with Christine for lunch, because she was always sitting with one of the managers or one of the other adults. Generally, I sat with the younger crowd John was hanging out with. There seemed to be a clear division of adults and young adults. Gabe sat with us since he was younger but he lived in town and didn't come up to volunteer every day, just usually on the weekends.

I started to dress in all white clothing. Nobody asked me to. I guess I was copying the Guru's style since I thought it was cool or holy or something. I set up my schedule to start meditating ten to twelve hours a day. Luckily the managers agreed to this. I would work for four hours in the garden—weeding, pruning, planting, raking, shoveling compost, and more weeding—and then I'd shower, grab a quick lunch, and hike up to the meditation cabin outside the main grounds—a twelve-minute hike outside the deer fence, and up the mountainside. I would use a road made of dirt and rock, and then cut back into the woods on a trail, and wind my way down to the cabin along a narrow path with small pebbles and weeds. Along the trail you had to watch out for the poison oak bushes. In the cabin, I found only a wood stove and cushions intended to be used while meditating. It was quiet there.

In these first days, I felt that I should commit all or nothing. I had to go for it and dive in. My intention was to meditate as much as I could, even all night long.

CHAPTER XIV

THE GURU

After a few weeks of living at the Ashram, they switched me to kitchen duty. I'd prepare salads for lunch. My favorite part of this new job was creating salad dressings. During meal times, everyone knew everyone, but the younger crowd still segregated themselves. It was almost as if the younger crowd and the older crowd lived in two different worlds. To me, our generation was "the cool kids," and the adults were the enforcers who were out of touch with reality. They seemed to be live boring rigid lives. I'm not sure exactly why I felt that way, perhaps because being young automatically separates you from adults, both physically and mentally. But at the Ashram, the adults seemed to be unified whereas, the younger generation felt like we were all on our own. So even though I was part of a group, the loner in me was still predominant.

I adopted Hindi words into my everyday conversations, and I began quoting the Guru on a daily basis. In fact, all conversations related to the practice of meditation. I don't think anyone did these things consciously, but we were reading a lot of books that had an intensive glossary of terms in order to understand the text. If you wanted to fit into the group, you had to learn the lingo. For example, my favorite word was *Samadhi*. There's no single word in the American language that defines Samadhi. The words *trance* or *bliss* don't suffice. Indian culture is rich with spiritual terms and definitions that take time to understand, both practically and intellectually. Life was peaceful at the Ashram. Tucked away in these hills, I spent my days working in the kitchen, which we called the *Langar*, another Indian word which basically means the same thing—a community kitchen in a place of worship. Adults substantially outnumbered us twenty-somethings. Most elders were solitary, isolated, and moody characters. They sometimes gathered in smaller groups of two or three, but they usually just sat alone and sometimes radiated a vibe, as if to say 'don't bother me.'

Like Axe, for example, who was an old, white-haired Irishman who looked like Santa Claus. He was Patrick's father and actually a nice guy, but he always sat alone outside, looking out over the valley beyond the hills. Most people were reluctant to sit next to him during meal time because of his stern, foreboding presence. People didn't know how nice of a guy he actually was, however. Axe liked me, because I was friends with his son.

Whenever I worked with him, Axe would always let me go early. Sometimes, Patrick and I sat with him, looking at the beautiful view of the valley more than each other. Occasionally the valley would fill with fog down below while we floated on an island in the clouds, isolated, surrounded by mountains and trees. The sunsets were usually magnificent, always profoundly silent.

Normally I would sit at a long table in the middle of the room inside the dining hall. My roommate, Prem, often joined me, and sometimes, Kompal, but more often than not she ate alone and preferring not to talk. She appeared to be brooding, tortured inside herself. I could tell that Prem liked Kompal, but he was too shy to say anything about it. Because relationships were not allowed, I didn't think he could say anything romantic, even if he wanted to. Still, if Kompal ate alone, Prem would usually join her. I would let them be and sit with Patrick or John or sometimes Gabe who came up on the weekends. If I was lucky I'd meet a new guest to talk to. People came to stay at the Ashram for a week or so on meditation retreats. The guests would always have interesting stories to tell, and that was our prime entertainment.

At least their stories were more interesting than anything going on at the Ashram. Life here was actually rather boring. We had no television, no newspaper, no internet, no magazines, no cell phone or cell phone service, no mental entertainment of any kind. The only books on the property were those printed by the organization, mostly the writing or transcriptions of talks given by the masters. The guests were the prime source of feedback from the outside world. We were cut off, out in the woods, completely isolated, surrounded by tall trees and miles and miles away from any form of civilization to speak of. We couldn't even walk to a store or watch TV.

The only place we could walk was deeper into the forest, usually alone. Sometimes special guests with experience and background on the path of the masters came and told profound stories. Once such incident happened in the Main House where I ended up living, when I met Bob. He was older. Bob had been around in the early days and had traveled abroad with Sant Thakar Singh. Bob was a big guy, blond and reminded me of Ivan Drago, but the American hippie version.

"I heard you were with the guru when he was attacked in Africa," I casually mentioned as we sat on the sofa around the main house. Bob was holding the book composed of the talks Sant Thakar Singh gave to the Africans on that tour.

"Yeah, I was," he lifted the book to show me the cover with a picture of Thakar Singh dressed in white surrounded by who appeared to be smiling attentive African elders in colorful traditional attire.

"If it's cool with you, would you mind telling me the story?"

Bob hesitated. He had told the story before while I was listening in a group.

"Maybe another time," he nodded and began to walk away.

I could see he was tired after a long day of working in the garden and wanted to rest. But he stopped, turned back and told me anyway.

"The long and the short of it is, we were doing a public program in Africa and there were five to six hundred people crowded into this rather large theater with a 700 seat capacity. During the talk, a local African voodoo cult leader entered the scene with about two dozen men dressed head to foot in red, with red turbans and red scarfs covering their faces. They looked very demonic. Later in the day the police found dead bodies buried around the group's compound," Bob laid emphasis on that last sentence.

He continued, "Everyone noticed when they walked into the hall because the talk had finished by that time. We were about to teach the meditation and initiate those students who wanted to learn the method. But these men had not been in the talk and therefore couldn't attend the initiation. That's when I noticed that there was this dark vibe in the air. I could see that these men were not there to learn meditation at all. The invaders rushed onto the stage. I stood in front of the Master to protect him. Some of the men climbed up into the rafters and were jumping down from above and others beat up the security. Everyone began fighting. The cult leader of their gang just sat in the back booth watching like a coward. It was all very dramatic. I fended off some of the men but one man reached for the Master's turban and ripped it off. Another man snatched the master's shoes so I chased that guy down. I don't think I really hurt him much, but was wailing away pretty good. Things were way out of control. I got a few broken ribs, and I got our Guru's turban back."

"Our group rose up against these guys and started fighting back once they realized what was happening. Say like fifty to sixty people started fighting. It was an all-out brawl. So now we couldn't do the initiation. The event was ruined. The leader of the gang ran away when the police finally showed up. The police knew what was going on. They knew that the leader of this gang has staged this attack and set this all up. So one of these guys in red fell down a bunch of stairs and was injured pretty badly with a broken leg. Then Sant Thakar Singh Ji walked down the stairs to the injured man and pulled some money out of his own pocket and said to a police man, give this to that man so he can go to the hospital. But the police refused and arrested the man and took him to jail."

"So, the next day the Master handed us some money and told us to go down to the police station and bail out the men who were taken to prison. At that time the prisons in Africa were really hard. There was no room to even lay down, you are shoulder to shoulder, sitting in a circle and there's a hole in the ground in the middle of the room where you defecate. It just wasn't a good place to be. We went over there but the police wouldn't let us bail them out. We tried several times. The police really wanted to arrest the leader, but the devil had fled Africa. They said they'd only let the prisoners go if we could exchange their leader. So that's that story."

"Wow, that is a crazy story man," I finally said.

"It was written up in the paper. The cult leader battles a guru. The press wasn't good for the rest of our tour. But I got a chance to save him, well… our guru doesn't really need to be saved, but I got a chance to protect him."

"That's cool. I mean, it was good that you were with him at that time. Who knows what would have happened if a different representative had been with him," I commented. "Absolutely wild!"

"Yeah man, Africa was a trip. It was all very wild. Do you know why it was so wild?"

"Why?"

"Because all kinds of astral stuff going on there. It's full of crazy astral entities with all the black magic and witchcraft stuff. This cult gang leader was a voodoo priest and was doing black magic shit. When his black magic wasn't working, he'd resort to physical violence."

Despite that incident the 1989 African Tour of Sant Thakar Singh was a huge success. He toured 12 countries and taught over 5,000 people the inner light and sound meditation.

This story made a strong impression on me. It gave me a sense of my Guru's compassion and his dedication to serving humanity. I came to feel utmost respect for him and began to understand how great he really was. Maybe most Americans are not capable of understanding the kind of spiritual energy that can walk behind the humble, culturally foreign appearance of an Indian saint like him. In his physical presence, one moment of eye contact can astound those who are receptive with an indescribable bliss, or a sense of stillness as if a burden had been lifted from your mind. To those who just hear about him by chance, while being conditioned by our consumer culture and stale religious traditions, he becomes someone to judge. That's how a lot of people reacted when I told them what I was doing. I remember some hippie chick going off on me for my desire to better my life. Eventually Sean had a similar mind set. They both thought I was doing something weird and didn't know how to relate. This reaction is quite understandable, since meditation mainly comes from the East and is a foreign idea. But instead of trying to understand or at least tolerate something that seemed foreign, outside their privileged American-spoiled-brat point of view, they resorted to backbiting and talking crap and I felt pretty judged.

But those who judge what they don't understand just don't see the bigger picture of what's happening. They stubbornly refuse to at least consider why an accomplished spiritual teacher like him does what he does. It doesn't help that there have been other foreign teachers who have come and fell short in one way or the other, only to get the rest of them stereotyped by the media as some sort of cult leader. In truth, my teacher was just like a volunteer who never charged any money.

Sant Thakar Singh was an elderly retired man who had enough money to live the last days of his life relaxing at home with his family. He didn't need to be traveling all over the world, offering to teach meditation for free. He never accepted payment from anyone who came to hear his talks or seminars. He came to share perhaps the best free gift anyone could ever receive. He dedicated himself to this service, what he knew to be the most noble and divine purpose of life. Why would someone do that? What's the motive? Who was he really, just some old man trying to make a buck? Nah.

It became clear to me that Sant Thakar was motivated by his compassion. His only desire was to alleviate the suffering of others by teaching others how to achieve moksha, or liberation. He understood the life changing transformative power of meditation and wished to share it with as many people as possible, for free. Because he had gained profound knowledge and inner illumination himself through his own meditation practice, he understood the benefit the practice could bring to individuals and humanity as a whole. World peace begins with inner peace. He traveled the world sharing the same gift and teachings that he accepted from his own Guru, Sant Kirpal Singh Ji, keeping the lineage of the Sant Mat teachings alive.

It was indeed a long lineage dating back to the 1500's. Sant Thakar Singh was spreading the same method taught by Guru Nanak Dev Ji (1469-1539) who was the first of the ten Sikh gurus. He was the first one in recorded history from India to have passed on this particular practice. Into the ancient past, Sant Thakar Singh has said, there have always been meditation masters on earth passing on methods to achieve inner enlightenment through both meditation and right actions. He has acknowledged Jesus Christ, among the others who have walked the earth and have been seekers of God, often quoting from John 1:14. "The Word became flesh and dwelt among us." Word God, according to Sant Thakar Singh, is another name for inner sound. The Buddhists call it intrinsic hearing.

The Sikh teachings became obscured and confused in modern times when the religion failed to realize the practical meaning of its own Adi Granth text, composed by the lineage of enlightened saints in verse, describing aspects of devotion, spiritual bliss and instructions on how to access to the inner spiritual planes. The essence of these sacred teachings gets lost over time and becomes misinterpreted when you don't have a realized spiritual teacher who practically understands the teachings. Book knowledge can help point the way, Thakar Singh would say, but it can't replace the highest knowledge and wisdom that is found within your own soul through meditation. "Half knowledge is dangerous," he would quote is own teacher. "An ounce of practice is worth tons of theory."

My teacher, who grew up in a Sikh family and for some time acted as a Sikh priest, ceased conforming to the conventions of his local temple after accepting the gift of meditation though Sant Kirpal Singh Ji. He kept it secret from the community, while practicing meditation on a daily basis for six months before telling anyone. When Sant Thakar

Singh Ji eventually became Kirpal's successor, a group of
Sikhs came to his house with swords drawn ready to kill
him. They were going to kill him because the religious followers of Sikhism blindly believed that there can be no
more living examples or Gurus after the tenth Sikh Guru
had died — the tenth Guru being the last and final one in
their belief system. They thought if someone pretends to be
a Guru he should be killed. But Sant Thakar Singh Ji spoke
to these men with love and kindness and they melted, putting down their swords.

The funny thing is that the Sikhs believe there is only
one God who is formless, timeless, and beyond any particular religion or belief system. And yet they believe their
belief system is the only one that is valid. Most religions
promote this elitist mentality.

`But the real goal is to realize the divine presence of
Oneness within oneself through intrinsic hearing, or Word
or Inner Sound. Shabd is also another word from India,
which means Inner Sound, a sound emanating from the
crown chakra. But the Sikhs had interpreted this to mean,
song. And so, the Sikhs sing songs in their temples and call
them Shabds. And because they won't listen to any other
authority on the subject, they've lost the essential meaning
taught within their very own religious text, which is a
common religious mistake. Their minds are so convinced
that they think they understand the real meaning, and thus
spread a false interpretation and the masses go along with
it. But the real understanding is always practical. This is
why I call myself a practical spiritualist. I'm not just going
to follow a blind belief that's been passed down for hundreds of years, but will test it out for myself, practically
speaking. If I can prove a theory is true, then I'll adopt it,
but only after I've tested it out.

Actually, the secret to the sound is that it emanates from
within your own soul. You can actually hear it coming
down from the top of your crown Chakra. This sound is in

fact the Shabd they talk about in their holy book the Guru Granth Sahib, which is the main holy religious scripture of Sikhism. The Sikhs regard this book as the final, sovereign and eternal Guru. And because that book is misunderstood by Sikhs, in the same way Christians fail to understand the real meaning of the Bible, both fail to realize the practical spiritual meaning behind the words in both books and waste their time because they're unable to practice what the book says.

Now Guru Nanak did promote the practice of Naam Simran, which involves the constant remembrance and meditation on the divine name or essence. By focusing one's mind on God and engaging in devotional practices, individuals can develop a deep connection with the divine and acquire spiritual wealth and gain entry into the 'Realm of Truth'. But the actual specifics of this practice have been forgotten, at least until now.

My teacher dedicated his life to teaching these practices, which were forgotten over time. How exactly do you develop an awareness of the divine presence of God within and around you? That is the mystery that my teacher had unraveled and passed along to his students. He had read the Sikh scriptures countless times, even taught them for years, but until he met his own Guru Sant Kirpal Singh, he also remained lost.

What exactly is so important about this practice of meditation? It facilitates a deeper connection with the consciousness that can be termed your soul, encouraging an awakening within of spiritual wealth that surpasses anything you could have ever envisioned or imagined. This awakening as soul gives you access to spiritual treasures beyond your most extravagant fantasies. The soul is often seen as the eternal part of a person that carries the core qualities, such as love, wisdom, and inner peace, which are not bound by the material world. When we speak of awakening the soul within this practical framework, we are referring to the meditative process of self-discovery and spiritual revolution that allows any individual to access and embody these core qualities consciously. This awakening involves moving beyond the superficial layers of identity shaped by societal and religious norms and to connect with the soul's innate purity and wisdom. This understanding is achieved through practice, and without practice, it can never be realized.

Collectively as a species, we've forgotten the true nature of our own soul. This speaks to a profound disconnection from our deepest essence and spiritual identity. This concept suggests that in the modern world, amid the rapid pace of technological advancement, the pursuit of material success, and the dominance of rational-empirical ways of thinking, humanity has drifted away from the intrinsic understanding of the soul as the core essence of our being. This disconnection manifests in various ways, impacting both individual lives and society as a whole. Many of society's problems stem from this identity crisis we are currently undergoing where everyone else seems to be to blame and the real solution remains shrouded in myopic mystery.

The human being carries a drop of consciousness from the Ocean of God – we can call that our soul. This is basic spirituality 101. The soul is distinct from the physical body and is of the same essence as the original divine nature of God. The soul is eternal and immortal, existing beyond birth and death. It is timeless, unchanging, and free from the limitations of the physical body. The soul possesses consciousness and self-awareness and it is the key to perceiving the divine link between ourselves and our Creator. Within the soul resides an inherent longing to know itself, for union with its source, the Supreme Being, God. It seeks to merge back into the divine source.

In the modern era, the emphasis on scientific materialism, consumerism, and external achievements has overshadowed the importance of spiritual values and inner growth. This shift has led to a collective amnesia regarding the soul's significance, reducing the human experience to physical and psychological dimensions alone. The soul, with its connections to the transcendent, the mystical, and the deeply intuitive, often finds little space in the narratives that dominate our understanding of what it means to be human.

Souls have come down into this world for mysterious reasons, the answers for which may not come to light until sometime along the way or at the end of the return trip. The practice of listening to the sound current, which emanates from the top of the head and following that sound is the most direct road to take. Through this inner spiritual practice, we attain authentic self-realization, and gain enough spiritual wealth to travel back to our original foundation, from where we first took birth into creation.

This is the secret of all religious texts and the one thing they overlook or don't make clear. It is important to say here that Sikhism, as a religion, does emphasize the practice of meditation but they fail to teach it to the followers at their temples, called Gurdwaras (doorway to the Guru). The importance of meditation is not stressed at their gatherings. I am not a follower of Sikhism myself, but have been to several Sikh temples and understand that the emphasis of the religion fails to convey the real spiritual practices within their holy book.

Sant Kirpal Singh Ji, and my Guru, while drawing inspiration from Sikh teachings, offered a specific approach to meditation that focused on the practice of Shabd Yoga or Sound meditation. They emphasized direct realization of divinity through the inner Sound, or the Word. It is written in the Bible, most notably right up front in the opening of the Book of John: "In the beginning was the Word, and the Word was with God, and the Word was God." The Sikhs also use the term Naam to name this creative force of Word

God, synonymous with or manifested as Shabd. Christians and Sikhs rely on their books to understand these spiritual terms. Despite numerous references to meditation, the single eye, and realizing oneself as God within, followers have not been properly taught how to worship the most useful reality of Word or Shabd resounding within them in any practical way. This is where spirituality turns into religion, and this is also the ultimate problem with not having a more practical understanding. The Bible even directly states that the human body is the temple of God. Despite these obvious statements, the actual practice has become obscured and is still misunderstood by almost everyone throughout the world.

Because I call myself a practical spiritualist, I don't believe something until I've seen it myself. If I could actually see God, I wouldn't need to believe in Him. The question of belief wouldn't arise in my mind. Belief always pales in comparison to experience. Thus far my experience proves this theory to be correct.

Christians ask themselves, what is God and can we have a personal relationship with Him? Within both of these religious texts, we can't find a direct answer through intellectual analysis. Knowing God is a practical matter. God can only be perceived but not intellectually understood or described. If this actual practice has been forgotten over time, then the underlying practical wisdom of direct experience would also be lost.

I wanted to approach these differences of religion and spiritual practice with an appreciation that spiritual paths can have diverse expressions and approaches. Ultimately, the spiritual path is a deeply personal journey, and individuals may find guidance in various traditions or from different teachers based on their own unique needs and inclinations. I want to emphasize here again that the real purpose of my Guru was to compassionately share spiritual understanding. To me it was important to see that the essence and precious secrets of most religions had been lost and forgotten. My teacher had come to reawaken the people, to help enable them to experience a vital, authentic, evolving, and enduring spiritual realization within themselves, and for that I respected him.

These thoughts helped me to press on and continue my practice of meditation for myself, in order to awaken my own personal experience of the Divine. And maybe finally I could answer the question, was it possible to actually see God with my own eyes, while my eyes were wide open? Is God real and not some dogmatic belief?

I had been living at the Ashram for eight months when an eighteen-year-old Russian named Vlad showed up, and I discovered that I wasn't the only young, hard-core meditator out there.

This dirty-blond haired Russian kid stood in line for food, along with the rest of us, and once he got his plate, he looked directly at me. I nodded to him.

"What's up," I said. I took my tray and went and sat down.

After Vlad got his food and looked around at all the adults scattered here and there, he came and sat next to Patrick, Prem, and me. Kompal was off on her own, and for some reason, Prem had decided not to sit with her that day. And John had also found a new love interest in one of the Ashrams new recruits, Sheila. Sheila worked in the garden and John and Sheila got married faster than I could realize that they were even dating. Which I thought was not allowed in the first place.

"Hey, nice to meet you," I beamed. "I'm Greg."

"My name is Vlad."

He said his name in a cool, low-key tone, with a hint of a Russian accent. When he said "Vlad," it sounded more like "Lad."

Prem introduced himself and then asked where Vlad was from.

"Colorado," Vlad offered. "Man, it's so great to be here. You have no idea," he changed the subject and looked carefully around the hall.

"Welcome to Wonderland," Patrick smirked, taking a bite out of his oatmeal cookie.

I laughed to lighten the mood. This got a slight smile out of Vlad. I looked at Patrick, then back at Vlad.

"Great place to meditate," I added. "Try to meditate as much as you can."

"I'll try," said Vlad, nodding.

He had a plate full of food, while my plate was almost empty. He would be eating for a while after I was finished, but I stuck around, because it wasn't every day that we had a new face at the meditation center.

Prem was naturally inquisitive, throwing questions at Vlad: "What's your story? What brought you to the Ashram? Why do you like the practice of Shabd Yoga?"

"Whoa, man," said Patrick. "Slow it down with the questions, amigo."

Living out in the woods, away from society with no television, phone, or any sort of entertainment, made us all naturally more talkative. Even the most stoic of us would crumble beneath the mental tedium and grab at an opportunity to talk to someone new.

After so many months, my natural enthusiasm for meditation had begun to falter. When I first arrived, I easily put in eight to nine hours of meditation a day. Now I would be lucky if I got in half that.

"Man, the world was driving me totally insane," Vlad said. "Can you believe it? I almost joined the Army! But then one day, I went to go and sign up, I found this flyer about awakening your soul, and I called the number. That weekend I went to a meditation initiation and got initiated. I was saved, man. Otherwise, I would probably be in boot camp right now."

"That's pretty wild," I said. "You dodged a bullet."

Prem nodded in agreement with a heavy exhale.

"Yeah," he said, "none of our parents really want us to be here. How about you? What do your parents think of this place?"

"My mom thinks I'm joining a cult," Vlad said. "But I would have gone crazy if I didn't come here. I need this right now. I felt like I was going crazy out there on my own. So, like, I didn't really have a choice."

"Fuck parents," Patrick said, indignantly.

His comment got a rise out of Vlad. Prem and I were both used to Patrick's sarcastic one-liners. He was always saying something controversial, blunt, or anti-establishment, to attract attention.

"Yeah, man, we've got to focus on meditation," Vlad continued. "That's what I really need at least. I don't know about you guys, but without this path, I don't know what would have happened to me."

"I'm in the same boat," I said. "I need to meditate like a fish needs water."

"Amen to that," Prem chimed in.

"Ah, man, I'm on dishes," said Patrick. "Nice to meet you. I'll catch you guys later."

He stood up and offered his hand to Vlad, who shook it.

"He looks pretty young," Vlad said to us, as he watched Patrick walk away.

"He's sixteen," I said.

"He's here with his father," Prem said. "It's pretty rare that someone as young as you comes to a meditation group like this."

"So, how much meditation are you guys getting in?" Vlad said, finally taking a bite of his salad.

"I was getting in about eight to nine hours a day for a while," I said, "but it's dropping off now."

"Whoa, man, that's amazing."

"I try to get in the recommended three hours," said Prem.

"I want to get in as much meditation as I can," Vlad said, nodding.

"Yeah," I grinned. "You came to the right place."

"We can't all be over-achievers like you," Prem said, smirking at me.

"If you guys want to come up to the meditation cabin with me, I could use some support," I said, taking the last bite of my sandwich.

"Yeah, count me in," Vlad said, enthusiastically.

"I'm just trying to maintain a balance," said Prem. He stood up. "You guys have fun."

"Balance is good, but it's nothing I'm good at," I said.

I put on an apron and joined Patrick at the dishwashing station. After thirty minutes, we finished doing everyone's dishes, drying them, and putting them away. When I walked outside, Vlad was sitting on the grass, watching the sunset.

"Have you read any of the books on Sant Mat?" I asked, as I sat down next to Vlad, referring to the Sant Mat spiritual path and its lineage of various Gurus.

"Ah, yeah," he said, a little self-consciously. "I like some of Kirpal's books."

"Have you read the passage about the four restraints?"

"I'll have to check it out. I don't know that one."

"Yeah," I said, "we can talk about that more sometime, if you want. Anyway, I'm going to go meditate. See you around."

"Later," said Vlad, waving.

I walked up to the meditation hall for the rest of the evening.

Life was simple at the Ashram. We meditated, ate, socialized, worked, and meditated some more. Sant Thakar Singh was coming to visit at the end of the summer, which started to draw a lot more people. That's why Vlad had come instead of joining the Army.

A little while later, my high school friend, Jeff, arrived to join the meditation retreat, too. He planned on staying through the rest of the summer until the Guru arrived. On one of my days off, Jeff and I went hiking deep in the woods.

We were cave hunting.

"So how did your time go at that Buddhist center?" I asked.

"I got kicked out," Jeff said.

"Really! What happened?"

"Well, when I was coming up here, I didn't tell them I was visiting another meditation center. They found out somehow. I think the main monk overheard me talking about it on the phone or something. She said that it wasn't okay for me to be practicing a different meditation method while living at her temple. Also, she felt like I lied to her since I didn't tell her about it."

"Man, that's brutal. So where are you gonna live?" I asked.

"Everything I own is in my car right now. So I came up here for three weeks to figure out what my next move was gonna be," Jeff smiled.

"Good plan."

After about an hour-long hike into the woods, miles from any trail or road, just wandering down deer trails and the ridge of this cliff, we spotted a large cave. I stayed on top of the ridge and he went below the ridge line. From my vantage point, I could see the cave, which was not apparent to him, so I told him which way to go.

I noticed there were a lot of leaves above the cave along the hillside, and there were depressions and paths in the leaves, which looked to me like someone or something had been walking to the cave.

Following my directions, as Jeff approached, I heard a cat growl.

"Jeff?"

He stopped moving, frozen. Then he ran.

I scrambled down the hillside. "What was it?"

"I think I just saw a mountain lion. But I'm not sure," he said, breathlessly. "In the cave, I saw two yellow eyes."

"What did they look like?"

"Well," he continued, "At first, I just saw the two eyes looking at me, so I got a little nervous. But then I looked again and the eyes were yellow, and then I really tried to focus. I looked a third time and they were cat eyes."

"You're right. It's probably a mountain lion," I said.

"I think so," Jeff said, still catching his breath.

"Maybe we should go?" I said, casually, but feeling nervous as hell.

"Yeah." Jeff said, nodding nervously, but keeping his voice totally under control. "I think you're right. Let's go." We fled back up the mountain ridge until we reached the gravel road. That would be our last cave hunting adventure for a while.

Jeff and I both shared an unhealthy confidence that nothing could hurt us because we both believed we we're protected by God and our guru. In Sant Mat the guru is seen as an embodiment of divine wisdom and has reached a level of God-realization most people would find it very difficult to reach. We believed that without our guru's grace, spiritual progress would be difficult. But the teacher often said that the real guru is within and the ultimate goal is for the student to attune to the inner God consciousness, which is the true, eternal Guru.

The outer teacher essentially acts as a bridge to connect the student to the inner divine source, leading us along the inward path towards self-realization and God realization. Thus while both are crucial, the "God within" is considered the ultimate teacher, the source of all spiritual knowledge and the pathway towards liberation. And not only that but this has also been true for thousands of years.

CHAPTER XV

SPIRITUAL WEALTH

For the rest of the summer, I avoided talking. "Keeping silence" is one way to avoid leaking any spiritual energy.

How does one avoid spiritual leakage? It's done by controlling the senses and exercising "the four restraints." I withdrew and didn't really talk to anyone while I just practiced meditation as much as possible. I was able to arrange my schedule so that I didn't have to go to lunch with everyone who liked to socialize. The only time I saw anyone was at breakfast. People began to ask where I was hiding.

"I've been going up to the meditation cabin," I answered, truthfully.

During my break time at work, I sat in the nearby meditation room inside the Octagon house, eyes closed, looking within my forehead to open my third eye, focusing the mind and the withdrawing the outgoing faculties.

Some days I packed a sandwich and skipped out to take the fifteen-minute hike up the hill to the meditation cabin. Few ever went there because it was inconvenient and too far out of the way. Some people were also afraid of bears because it was outside the fence. Going to the cabin was more like an entire day's event. I never saw anyone up there, except on occasion, a German man named Holgar. Although my conversations with Holgar were always brief, they were also always memorable. He'd always say something wise with a sly grin.

During my intensive meditation sessions, I began to hear the Sound Current coming through the top of my head, or the Crown Chakra. It wasn't a physical sound, but a spiritual vibration manifesting as energetic life force that can both be heard and felt. The more I listened with concentrated attention, the more I could merge into it. I began to absorb this spiritual energy into my soul and started to realize the distinction between soul and mind.

But alas, I always craved more. I thought about what this hunger for the highest self-realization through meditation might have in common with the hunger for the food. Everyone gets hungry right? But few people seem know what spiritual hunger feels like. Most have become numb. I thought perhaps the innate craving for spiritual food hides behind all the thoughts and desires to enjoy one's life — looking for satisfaction in relationships, material comforts, possessions — constantly looking outside for satisfaction. When the real solution was to look within for the answers. But to change this outward habit proved to be quite rough.

I tasted some inner elixir that summer, and a new persistent hunger for it boiled in my heart. I needed it like a drug addict needs his fix. I was obsessed. Getting this soul food felt like total relief. Apparently, my drug episode in high school had left me like a thirsty man in the urban desert, but within I found an oasis. I'd been forced to find a solution to heal and revive my tortured soul. I thought that despite all the distress I'd gone through, I was actually lucky for that wake up call. That's just the way it worked out for me. I understood that many, if not most people, might never stop to look for what exists within the still silence of their own awareness.

Who am I? I would ask myself.

At first, this question made me go bananas, because this question didn't seem to have an answer. I felt anxious whenever I thought about it. I mean, *who the fuck am I?*

I am suffering, yeah, but *what* is suffering so badly?

I couldn't blame anyone for this anguish. This was my riddle to solve. I came to the Ashram to meditate, and with sincere effort the regular practice began to quench my thirst and satisfy my spiritual hunger. I developed a genuine sense of who I am. Finding the inner candy to satisfy that aching pang in my soul, at last I felt some relief. Until this point, I had been a broken man, splintered and shattered, like Humpty Dumpty.

Vlad asked me one day about the four restraints.

I explained, "When we restrict the outward flow of attention, we gain inner strength to rise within. We do this by listening to the Inner Sound with presence of mind — the real essence and first primal manifestation of consciousness — heard not with the physical ears, but through transcendental hearing. This practice of mindful listening involves full attention on the sound, without distraction. The mind gets distracted easily and must be reminded like a school child who needs incentive to remain quiet and attentive. I call this practice returning to focus or refocus for short. As more divine elixir rains down, the mind naturally becomes pacified. Then, withdrawn completely within, the attention effortlessly absorbs the sound."

"The more elixir you gather within by staying empty, the more content you'll feel. In order to disentangle our soul from our ego, we direct our focus inwards through the process of hearing within and maintaining four restraints. As our soul regains its original strength, the mind stills. This is the inner practice.

But what is the outer practice?"

The Four Restraints

• *Limit Speech and Physical Interaction (talk less).*

• *Control Seeing (spend more time focusing on what you see or sense within your Third Eye in meditation, avoid excess outside visual impressions).*

• *Limit Hearing (practice Intrinsic Hearing and listen to the sound that emanates from within).*

• *Restrict Thinking (focus your mind in the present moment, and then remind yourself again to refocus all day long).*

During this time period, I practiced these four restraints religiously. When you diet, you curb your appetite and eat smaller portions. It's not always easy. You'll feel hungry. In the same way on the spiritual quest, you realize that the impressions coming in through the eyes and ears, generate thoughts, which stir up the unsettled the mind.

When I followed the four restraints, I had more spiritual experiences, and my 3rd eye stayed open allowing for more spiritual energy to gather inside.

Along with following these guidelines I also tried to stay present all day long. When I was doing something, I remained aware of what I was doing without allowing my mind to wander. At first my attention was scattered and I had a hard time focusing, but then I'd begin to gather my awareness and increase my ability to concentrate. If my mind wandered I'd refocus by asking it a simple question or giving it a direct command, like: No thinking.

As my steady mind became more absorbed in meditation, I began to trust the process and increase the velocity of energy flow by going deeper for longer periods of time. The more I practiced, the more I was able to trust the process and having a concentrated mind became habitual.

By restraining speech, we avoid scattering our energy with our words. When you are constantly spewing out thoughts the subtle influence of ego is never far away. The responses of others mix to create more spin and lingering impressions on the mind, taking your focus away and diluting the concentration needed for a deeper meditation practice. Silence is golden. By sitting in meditation with my eyes and ears closed without moving around much all day, my mind became hungry and I began to crave stimulation. My mind was getting desperate, wanting to rebel. Nevertheless, like on a diet, I restrained those urges. I pushed myself. I kept my eyes and ears closed, controlled my mind, and persevered on my quest like Don Quixote.

I set out to prove to myself that the life of my soul was not hopelessly lost. I embarked on my own hero's journey, a quest to cross the far shore and enter the beyond while still alive. All barriers and obstacles on the way were my foes. I'd left my ordinary world, followed the sirens call to enlightenment, heeding advice from my mentors. I battled to cross the threshold of the matrix, my thoughts constantly betraying me. But the mind and the senses persist—they keep coming back in new disguises!

When you want to earn money, you have to work for that paycheck. In the same way, there's a spiritual currency that we gain through meditation. It accrues the same way money does, by hard work, time, and making deposits. If you want riches, spiritually speaking, hard work is the first key. The second key is making deposits into your spiritual bank account.

Although we are just comparing financial wealth to spiritual gains, riches are still something you must first acquire and then learn to manage. How you manage your money directly correlates with how you work at keeping your spiritual wealth. Let's say you do a ten-day meditation retreat, chances are you'll feel great, and experience the benefits of all of that hard work. You sat on your meditation cushion for hours, quieting your mind and developing your faculty of concentration. You accumulated a certain feeling of peace that you can now take with you once you go home. This is the same spiritual wealth you take with you when you die.

But if you do not maintain a healthy meditation practice afterwards, after a few days, weeks or months, you'll again fall back into feeling how you felt before you went on the retreat. All of your gains will be lost, all your wealth drained. Therefore, management is required, restraint advised, and discipline is a must. To navigate the path of spiritual self-sufficiency, we must identify and cultivate behaviors that support both self-esteem and spiritual growth. I used to believe that motivation would find me. But through introspection, I was able to foster a sense of integrity and my motivation blossomed naturally.

This wasn't some cosmic prank. I had pristine faith, and got a surge of pure grade A motivation and was ready to high tail it out of this reality and into the realms beyond. I wanted to rocket past the ghost world in the astral plane where most souls wander empty and aimless.

If you still believe you're a human being when you die, that belief is a ghost in your mind. None of that bullshit for me, I was aiming for the realm of the God beyond the Gods, spiritual regions beyond the pull of the ego driven by desires and karma, putting to shame any notion of a Heaven existing in the Astral plane. Nah, I was marching up that stairway to the highest inconceivable heaven, like a shooting star heading for that Supreme reality only a handful have ever glimpsed, the eternal realm of God! No way I'd get snagged in some sub-astral heaven where I'd be moping about looking like my human form in the astral body—separate from the realm of the One and clueless about what real God consciousness is.

I'd done my homework, drawn up a theory and set my

sights on what I perceived to be practically attainable. If anyone was gonna do it, it'd be me. I just wanted to sync my headspace with that invisible reality, beyond all the noise, kicking back in meditative mode to reach escape velocity on auto-pilot. I would get on that one-way Willie Wonka infinite elevator.

Excitement pulsed! However, my enthusiasm contrasted with the fellow seekers at the Ashram, who seemed to be stuck in their daily grind. Except for another loner.

Holgar, the tall German also sat there for long hours and usually stayed until midnight. I once went into the meditation communal room down in the village at three in the morning and he was still there meditating, sitting up straight like an immovable mountain. It seemed like he never slept. The man was a God of discipline, and the king of Sparta, if Sparta set out to conquer the soul.

It was around four in the afternoon, when I took a break and sat on the deck of the meditation cabin, smoke coming out of the chimney, eating some snacks I'd prepared. My hair was long and I hadn't shaved in a few days. I was wearing white pants and a white t-shirt with no shoes looking like some average American hippie dude whom you might bump into at a yoga studio. Holgar stepped outside to take a short breather from an all-day meditation binge. He had also prepared something to eat as well and we both sat for a few minutes looking at the peaceful scene.

Holgar, leaning in like a dude who just found some ancient, sunken treasure of gold, got that look in his eyes like he knew something I didn't. "This book," he began with a thick German accent, "It's legit. Want to crank your productivity to the max? This is your ticket. It's yours."

As we looked out over the beautiful valley below, feeling a cool wind and the warmth of sunlight, kicking back outside that cabin, enjoying the view of the rolling grassland, tall trees and the sky-blue Umpqua River winding its way through the mountain pass down below, I leafed through the pages of the book Holgar had just handed me, titled 'Seven Habits of Highly Effective People'. He began speaking about his personal process and how he's mixing up the seven habits techniques into his own meditation style, creating a new paradigm shift.

The guy's no couch potato. Well, when he sat for hours, he wasn't looking at an electronic screen, he was looking inside, all the time. He meditated like a robot, cranking out insane hours every damn day, day after day like an unstoppable monk machine. It's beyond wild and I was in absolute awe of this meditation monster sitting next to me. That intensity left a strong mark on my practice.

Just sitting there, next to him, and soaking it all in, feeling the vibes of that beautiful landscape, I said, "It feels like the universe is giving us a nod, you know what I mean?"

"Yeah, I do Greg!" he said. "Let me explain how I started. First, I built up my meditation time. It wasn't easy, but my commitment to the practice was my priority. In doing so, I found that the initial stages were about discipline. I noticed a subtle shift in my daily consciousness after that, as if meditation created a continuous stream always flowing in through my head and out my third eye."

Holgar continued, detailing the transformative effects, "The increased duration allowed me to delve into the subtle layers of consciousness. It was as if my mind expanded within the space of meditation. Thoughts that once seemed like walls, vanished, and the ebb and the sound anchored me in the present moment and my mind stopped all together."

He emphasized the importance of consistency, "But the key is not telling your mind what you're going to do. Discipline alone won't work. The mind will most definitely rebel like a wild horse, kicking and screaming. So you have to make friends with the mind."

"How do I do that?" I asked.

"One of the skills you need is what our teachers call 'Far

Sight'. It's about envisioning your ultimate goal. Keeping the end in mind and understanding where you're going so it just becomes second nature. Applying this to meditation, I started to see my practice not just as a daily routine but as a journey into the realm of the Gods, which would eventually lead me to the God beyond all the other Gods."

"God beyond God sounds amazing, but is it real?"

Holgar's eyes gleamed as he elaborated, "Use the ideas of the Circle of Concern and the Circle of Influence in your "Seven Habits" book. The author, Stephen Covey, explains how focusing on what you can control — your Circle of Influence — rather than getting distracted by external concerns beyond your sphere of influence will significantly impact your effectiveness. 'The Circle of Influence' comprises only the aspects of our lives we can directly impact."

"In meditation, I channeled this by concentrating on the aspects I could directly influence: my schedule, time I sat for meditation per day, and my prayer sessions to channel the highest possible grace quotient."

"Grace quotient, right on," I nodded. "Sounds cool."

Closing our conversation as we were about to go back into the meditation cabin, he smiled and said, "Remember, don't forget the seventh habit, 'Sharpen the Saw.' Holgar's passion for the subject was contagious. "Daily practice is your bread and butter. Don't lose your gains. Stay hungry and get rid of the rigamarole."

So, there I was, diving into the whole Circle of Concern vs. Circle of Influence thing, laying it all out on paper. I wrote down every damn activity, every task, like I was mapping out an elaborate robbery to steal back my soul. I scheduled my life like a ruthless strategist, axing any second wasted that didn't vibe with my main game plan to get a natural high – leveling up my effective meditation time.

I was like Tom Cruise in Mission Impossible. On the move, hitting the next task with perfect aim, and every crossed-off task being a little victory. And a series of little victories lead toward the powerful force my friend Bryan called momentum.

But Holgar was right, or seemed to be so at the time, that the key to staying motivated was "keeping the end in mind." As I delved into the depths of a ten-hour meditation day, it was hard to remain nostalgic and maintain that level of hyped momentum. Part of me wanted to cut my losses.

And to top that off, maintaining this heightened level for weeks on end was intolerable, but moments of profound stillness made it worth it. All I had was moments. I experienced a beauty that I can't begin to explain. It was like glimpsing into a favorite painting and watching it come to life, where the boundaries between the self and the universe begin to blur and all the remains is life itself.

On an earlier occasion, on a meditation break I sat with Holgar on the cabin's porch, the forest stretching out below us. The setting sun painted the sky in pink, reminding me of Miami.

"Can I ask you something?" I began. "Can you explain the concept of a spiritual bank account? I get it, but…"

His eyes twinkled. "Life's a game. In the game of life, your avatar can earn two types of currency: coins and gems."

I listened, intrigued.

"The first coin," he continued, "is like video game money. You earn the coins in game, and can use 'em to buy items in the game - houses, clothes, weapons. But when you turn off the game, those coins disappear. They don't transfer to life outside the game."

"And the gems?" I prompted.

"Ah, the gems are special, harder to earn. They're a real world asset like crypto currency. It's hard to understand at first, but you can send those gems out of the game and spend 'em in the real world. That's spiritual wealth."

The metaphor clicked. "So in life, our material possessions and cash are like the coins in your analogy…"

"Exactly," Holgar nodded. "Your car, your job, your bank balance – they're all in game coins. Important for playing the game we call life, but ultimately, after death these coins vanish, you can't take anything with you."

"And spiritual wealth, that's the gem," I mused. "Meditation, self-awareness, compassion."

Holgar smiled. "Now you're getting it. But let me give you another example. Think of your favorite song. That song, it's just vibrations in the air. But it can make you feel nostalgic or sad. It can inspire or comfort you. That's what spiritual wealth is like. It's intangible, but its effect is real."

A gentle breeze rustled the leaves above. I closed my eyes, suddenly aware of something - that something was that the invisible energy I've been focused on was..."

"You know Greg," Holgar offered, "you know where the real wealth actually is. That's why you come up here every day. You sit here in the cabin looking for it. This awareness, this sound, this spiritual music that's energy - it's like those gems. The more you listen, the more gems you collect, no one can ever take 'em from you. You take 'em with you wherever you go. The people out there in the city beyond the mountain, they got no idea what they're missing out on. But you, you know where the real gems are."

Something opened and my brain sparked, seeing the world as the ultimate opportunity, an opportunity like none other. I felt a shift, as if up until this point I'd been looking at the world through the small intellect of an Ai-NPC, like seeing out a foggy window and someone had just wiped it clean and uploaded a new operating system that had no firewall.

"So when we meditate," I said aloud as if in a dream, piecing it together as I went, "we're not just sitting..."

"Were banking gems brother," Holger finished my sentence with a grin. "We're investing in the only real currency that truly matters. The currency of consciousness."

We continued meditating for several hours. As it got

dark, I felt that shift that occurs when you spend the entire day in meditation. The abstract concept of meditation suddenly made sense, not just as an idea. And for the first time, I began to grasp why I came here. I realized then that this was what I'd been searching for all along. Not to escape from my old life, but to find a new way of seeing it. And for the first time, I felt grateful for being alive.

In stillness, I became aware of a subtle vibration. At first, I thought it was just the blood rushing in my ears. But as I focused on it, it grew stronger. It was a sound, but unlike anything I had heard before, a celestial audible hum that seemed to resonate with every cell in my body.

With a jolt of wonder, I recognized this must be the Shabd, the cosmic sound current that my teachers spoke of. It wasn't just a metaphor or a poetic description, it was real, alive, a life force and I was both hearing and absorbing it.

As I let myself dissolve into this sound, the boundaries of my body began to blur. I had a dizzying sensation of expansion, as if I was spreading out to fill the entire room, the entire forest, the entire universe. In this expansive state, I caught a glimpse of something vast and luminous, a presence and consciousness that I instinctively recognized as divine, as holy, as pure and pristine as God. It was God.

For a moment that felt like an eternity, I was suspended in this state of pure awareness. There was no Greg, no ashram, no Earth, just God consciousness, just being.

Holgar's advice lingered. He was a true testament to the transformative power of commitment and the boundless potential that lay within the depths of a hardcore meditation practice. In some ways I felt like Holgar was my real teacher. He was a pragmatic German perfectionist, using the 7 Habits methodology and applying that to achieving spiritual success, he did what very few people on earth have ever been able to accomplish. Inspired by his pristine example, I pushed myself to the limits and followed his scientific approach, reaching a point where I no longer felt like I was living in the real world.

In my quiet moments, surrounded by the stillness of that cabin in the woods, I was determined to distill the essence of meditation into a formula for success. Then I would take that formula and apply it like Holgar had done.

As an afterthought, I stumbled onto this revelation that being too laser-focused on planning was also messing with my head. It hit me, like a flashback to the wisdom from the Beginner's Mind Zen center. They casually mentioned that enlightenment wasn't like the lottery; it wasn't a distant prize but something to snag right here right now. The moment was always now. But I was planning, thinking, and daydreaming. What I was noticing were subtle the oscillations of my mind. I would mull my plans over like a chore a little too much. How about I just abandon plans themselves? Just follow a schedule and not bother about it.

How did I do this and stay focused, you ask? Well, I cooked up a term I call "directed beingness." Yes, I made up that word.

Once you're walking on the path, you ditch the map. No need to obsess over where you're headed. Because you already know where you're going, you can just let go and be. Sure, aim for a finish line, but just relax. Focusing on the goal too much became another tricky illusion of the mind, keeping me stuck in a maze of conceptions and daydreams.

As I forgot about the future goal, I remembered to trust the moment and just focus. I was moving moment to moment. Life is pretty easy. All I needed to do was stay focused in the moment, because the present moment is the magic sauce that made meditation work anyway. Staying in that groove, my meditation transcended to the next level. I entered the 4th dimension. I leveled up by forgetting to level up. Focusing here and now poofed out the noise in my head like a magic trick, and let me tell you, my reality became a four dimensional kaleidoscope of intoxication.

My consciousness bled into another reality and deep in

the vibe of directed beingness, I could just be, no distractions and the circle of confusing irrelevancies in the web of amorphous thoughts subsided. All that remained was perfect Zen. When I walked, it was no longer me walking.

Many people seem to think more about spending, or they certainly must spend more money than they save. If trends in money spending correlate to how our spiritual assets dissipate, then it's not hard to imagine how even those who meditate regularly fail to become spiritually rich. Some may even be practicing meditation because they knowingly or unknowingly use the profits of enhanced mental focus to become more successful, comfortable, well-traveled, and ultimately bound to this world. One of the biggest tricks of the mind is spending spiritual wealth to appear fashionably enlightened in the eyes of others. I guess you could say I'm doing that by writing this book.

It's been said that the subtle yet ruthless Ego of the Mind is the last thing to go. Of course, if the meditation time slacks and the outward faculties reign, the squandering mind and senses lay it all to waste, and you end up short handed anyway. On this road, the way was slippery.

I don't think most people know that spiritual wealth exists. The concept is totally foreign. Quite possibly, reading these words may seem odd. The idea of collecting spiritual wealth is something that I hadn't fully cognized until I first noticed how it helped me cope with my depression.

Everyone's heard the phrase: "You can't take it with you (when you die)." You already knew that; it comes as no surprise. That's why people write wills. But to think about taking your spiritual wealth with you after death could be a head scratcher. These concepts are almost exactly the same, but in reverse. It finally sunk in that the purpose of life here was working for the celestial currency. This may not be as far-fetched to understand as you think.

If only one person in the entire world saw the Truth, and the rest of the world was blind, no one would believe that person. But… if there was some evidence, then people might possibly believe. For myself, I could find no better evidence than my own personal experience. I didn't really want to write this book. But I know direct experience is king. And I felt compassion for the misfortune of others. I'd overcome depression and realized a new pathway no one was following. I felt like I had to say something.

"On a dark night, the far-off flicker of light helps one's onward journey, so does the sound and the inner light help the soul in its silent, solitary upward journey to its source, the True home of the soul," wrote Sant Kirpal Singh Ji.

"It can be said with certainty that the souls that descend into the regions of dissolution (Earth) and then ascend to the highest region by the grace of God are superior to the souls residing in the upper regions," wrote Sant Sawan Singh Ji.

"The world is filled with so much suffering. Let us practice Compassion and Love to be truly on the path of divinity." Swami Paramahansa Prajnanananda

CHAPTER XVI

WHERE GOD DWELLS

Later that summer, I gained a lot of momentum. The benefits from the intensive meditation retreat were compounding interest. I was working hard on that illusive goal of enlightenment, patiently praying for a breakthrough, perpetually hungering for a taste of *God Realization*. Was it an actually possibility? I still wasn't sure.

But with certainty, I knew I was gaining spiritual wealth, while jointly focusing on how not to lose momentum. Remembering what Holgar said, "don't lose your gains," I gradually became more efficient at staying in a conscious space feeling closer to God on the daily.

Then when I was meditating in the late afternoon up at the cabin, it came time to come down for lunch and prepare to catch the Guru's eight pm video. My self-imposed regimen, barely missing a full day of twelve hours in meditation for a span of two months, had induced a sensation of floating in limbo between this world and the next. If it's all an illusion, why get caught up in holding onto something that isn't even real?

As I walked down the path, the notion arose that my mind was like the surface of a pond. It was a simple thought that itself created ripples and made me look up at the horizon in a clear focused state. I felt like I had just witnessed a paradox. I began to witness my mind in this thoughtless state. And as each thought arose, making ripples, blurring my calm and peaceful state, I would stop the next thought from arising. Thus for a moment I gained control of my thoughts. Again, I'd return to the clear empty mind, a still pond. As I witnessed this, I thought that if the pond were completely still, the mind would become empty and clear like a mirror, so clear that it would reflect the ultimate Truth.

As I walked, I began repeating the phrase, "My mind is a mirror," and within seconds I could see each thought in my mind arise and disappear with ease. The still pond or mirror are just metaphors of course, just ways to communicate with my subconscious mind, and the only way I can think of to explain it. And then, in my empty state I wondered if I could push this stillness even further, what if I was the mirror itself? I stopped thinking altogether and looked out at the world, as if I was a mirror and no thoughts could penetrate my reflection. And in that moment, what did I reflect?

In the stillness of that moment the ego vanished, giving way to the pure inspiration, grace, and perfection of the Creator Himself.

I had become the soul who sees within and without, the transparent eye of perception itself and non-perception at the same time. It was no longer me who was the perceiver or the perceived. My old self ceased to be. My mind became as pure and still as a mirror. And as that happened, I wondered, what does a perfect mirror see?

In that moment, *I saw God and only God*.

The experience only lasted several seconds. With my eyes wide open, I perceived God everywhere and in everything. The awareness of the one Supreme reality circulated through me. It was like waking up from the dream that had been my life up to that moment. As quickly as the experience came to me, though, it vanished.

I knew I should have been grateful, but I what I felt was desperation. I wanted it to keep it, to live in that consciousness all the time.

I feared that I'd never have that kind of experience again. A monumental, almost traumatic sense of loss overcame me. I was immediately attacked by my own confused thoughts: What would happen to me now? How could I ever be happy again, or even want to meditate again? It was so difficult getting to the point of those few seconds. If I had to start from the beginning, I just couldn't do it!

I tried to calm down and think sensibly. Walking down the mountain after another meditation session. What did I do? I was thinking about my mind and about how quiet it was after so much meditation. I had repeated the phrase, "My mind is a mirror." I had tried to make my mind even more quiet and silent — like a mirror. I began to stop thinking entirely, only reflecting the world around me. I had become a reflection of the world itself. I had made myself disappear by reflecting reality. My final thought was, "If I was nothing more than a reflection, I wouldn't exist; only God would exist." Then I felt as if my mind really was a mirror. And there was a moment where I slipped through that magic mirror into God's domain.

If the mind could become perfectly still, it would reflect whatever was around it. I wouldn't exist apart from the Universe. Walking down the mountain, looking at the tall trees, passing a small pond, what I discovered in that still reflection was none other than the absolute Creator.

God filled every atom, every cell. He filled all the evergreen trees on the horizon. I could see it with my eyes wide open. As I looked at these distant trees, for the first time in my life I felt awake. And just as I came to this realization, just as suddenly as it began, the experience ended.

The whole thing lasted, possibly, only a few seconds.

And the bizarre, unexpected side effect?

The experience left me emptier than before. I now felt as if I were living in a dream world, and I was a dreamer who had just received confirmation—who now knew, *absolutely*, that he was trapped in a dream world. The feeling of anti-climactic disappointment came with the knowledge that my life was nothing more than an insubstantial passing dream.

Would I be able to experience God in meditation again? I didn't know. A new wave of melancholy washed over me. I wasn't depressed in the same way that I was before, but this time I just lost all motivation to meditate.

Have you ever seen the television series, *Buffy the Vampire Slayer*? I was left with a feeling similar to that of the title character after she returned from Heaven. In the program, Buffy tells her friends, "Wherever I was, I was happy, at peace. I knew that everyone I cared about was all right. I knew it. Time didn't mean anything. Nothing had form but I was still me, you know? And I was warm. I was loved. And I was finished. Complete. I don't understand theology and dimensions, but I think I was in Heaven. And now I'm not. Now... Everything here is hard and bright and violent. Everything I feel, everything I touch, this is like a fake dream world. Just getting through the next moment, and the one after that, knowing what I've lost...."

I could relate to Buffy because that was how I felt.

It may seem silly to relate a profound realization to a television show, but what, in fact, is reality? Is life like a television show with you as the main character? Is your life just a series of moving pictures that disappear once we turn off the T.V. and die?

If I could manage to glimpse reality beyond this dream with my eyes wide open—even catch a glimpse of God—then return to the dream world in which I live, would I live as a ghost? Could I accept a life that wasn't real? I didn't know and I didn't have any answers.

So I kept pressing on. In the early hours, when the light was just beginning to touch the edges of the mountains above meditation center, I would wake up, shower, and often sit to meditate, contemplating the vast, unspoken truth of our existence. It was hard to find at first, but I just kept meditating, looking within through the weeds of my thoughts and it was always there. This Truth, as I came to understand it, was simple yet profound: so much of the angst and frustration we go through in life is the consequence of being disconnected from our Creator, and the angst of separation becomes the very catalyst to drive rapid spiritual evolution. Once you catch a glimpse of the awesome reality of Him or Her, that over-riding inner knowledge holds great meaning and importance, feeding motivation for your continued life here and into the beyond.

I was becoming a man of action, unwilling to wait for death before understanding the mysteries of the afterlife. In the quiet solitude of the forest on the mountainside, I began to see Him, through the inner doors of perception, to be ever-present and eternal. It didn't happen at all once, not even every day, but on occasional short visits. In good time, to a greater or lesser degree, I would realize the clear connection to the source of salvation, on step at a time.

Throughout history, very few people can say they've seen God, but based on my experience, I can say God is real. There's a distinct difference between feeling God's presence and being one with the energetic force we call God. In order to be one with God, you have to eliminate your ego. That's when you'll see that only God exists. Once you erase yourself, only God remains. To become is to know. I don't need to believe in God, because I've seen Him. This is a deeply personal experience that has given me some insight into this subject, but I also know there is more to learn and am always open to growing in understanding.

The knowledge that requires transcendence is the hardest to come by. How many people through out history have said they've become one with God? I also admit that I feel some pride in this accomplishment, because no one can shake my faith since I've seen the truth directly. But this is not something I can't really take credit for as it is all the grace of the Supreme Creator and was an undeserved gift.

'The Way' to this understanding only comes from practical application. My story relates the importance of going beyond the science of observation, beyond the faith of feeling, to actually embody a real life subjective experience through practical application. When practice meets understanding, real knowledge unfolds.

The king of all wisdom is direct experience. We must live it to learn it. To perceive that force which is invisible to the naked eye, but unmistakable to the soul, is only possible through practical spirituality and following 'The Way'. Books inform, but life transforms. We do not need a path to follow, but a way to become.

Present minded awareness is the key to unlock the link between this physical holographic universe and our true essential nature. When we attune our minds to this present moment, our awareness mirrors Truth beyond the veil and as we begin to embrace the eternal essence of our soul.

If I can admit my blindness towards the avoidance of seeing this truth, then the path towards clarity will be easier. But if I lose myself, I lose my way and slip into the shadows of unconsciousness; what world do you think I'll be living in? So I need to be true to Truth.

I invite you on this journey of profound self-discovery. By embracing the truth you unlock the potential for transformation and for building a more fulfilling life. Look within and you will discover a deeper understanding.

CHAPTER XVII

THE WAY

Here in our physical world, we are like children lost in a forest, unable to see the path home. The spiritual teacher's true purpose is to help us fix this disorienting blindness and to realize that life presents a profound opportunity. In the struggle to find the way to our spiritual home, in the very act of seeking through meditation, we move upward, we ascend and transcend the bonds of forgetfulness.

The mystic appears as our personal guide or friend, pointing the way, but it is up to us to open our inner eye.

In the afterlife, as I've come to understand it, it is very easy to feel the presence of the Creator. But many, if not most of the souls who only identify as human bodies, become lost in the mazes of their self-concepts, losing the deeper connection to the universe. Once your body dies, you cannot take it with you. So why identify with yourself as a body, man or woman, if it's already gone and buried. What would become of you in the afterlife? You would merely be a shell of the mind, a ghost mind, with no awareness of who you really are as soul.

These ghosts believe so deeply in the idea of their body and are so completely entrenched in their non-existent past that their inner light of divine wisdom remains obscured as they wander the earth in despair with no hope of salvation.

Caught up in these mental projections of themselves, so deeply conditioned, they end up creating their own reality in the world beyond. This is because the reality you believe in is the reality you project over there. This is true both in the physical world as well as the spirit realm. The mind projects its own limited reality like a waking dream.

I had been lost in my own self-loathing, but when I came to the crossroads of self discovery, I took the road less traveled that leads to the land of truth and I journeyed alone out of my own self induced darkness.

When I say we are part and parcel of the universe, I mean it quite literally. We are the universe made conscious. We wake up to find out that we are the eyes of the World, the Universe, or God even, looking at itself.

Clinging to the idea of 'me' and 'mine', blinds us to the fundamental impermanence of existence. In our post-modern world, the hypnotic focus on scientific materialism and worldly wealth overshadows the mysteries that lie just beyond that veil of common understanding.

To only trust what we can see, touch, or measure with our five senses closes ourselves off to the vastness of the universe's hidden truths we can access through direct personal experience within our very own awareness. Awareness is in fact that which gives life to our five senses.

The knowledge of Quantum Physics, revealing that within the protons, neutrons, and electrons composing all matter there is only space and the minutest elusive energetic particles that behave temperamentally upon observation, gives us hints about the illusion of reality created here on earth. But still, this knowledge derived from sophisticated scientific instruments cannot help us see for ourselves. We neglect to realize our own sixth sense and open our inner eye of wisdom through our very own being.

The reality of death tells a different story. It reminds us that we're not the permanent, unchanging entities we believe ourselves to be. We are not Gods. Our bodies, our thoughts, our very selves are transient. Bodies die. They come into being, exist for a time, and then cease to be. This realization, though unsettling, is also liberating. It frees us from the illusion of believing in physical permanence. To me, it would be a nightmare, to be imprisoned in this holographic universe.

Through meditation and by following the advice I received from my spiritual mentors, I've come to see that embracing our impermanence is the first step in understanding this mystery. It's the motivating force driving us to ask questions. We're much more than bodies and collections of memories. When we die what can we take with us, truly, our mental photographs? We're fragments of the universe, conscious and connected to a network so vast we cannot even begin to comprehend the scope or limit of it.

Our journey back to our creator, our journey that transcends our earthly existence and the illusory boundaries of a self we imagine to be real, is *the Way* we must all follow. Honestly, there is no other option other than ignorance.

It's a peculiar irony that in the world beyond, where the presence of the Creator is so manifest, some lost souls are still unable to perceive Him at all. Yet in this world, where His presence is just a faint whisper, it's possible to catch a glimpse of the divine. All you need is the right tools to open your inner eye to see this Truth for yourself. Those rare moments, fleeting and precious, are the indications on the way of real awakening.

That's why, I believe, it's crucial to make even the smallest progress in this life. The work we do here, the understanding we gain, and this inner connection with the divine, however minute, sets the stage for our journey into the beyond after this life. In the afterlife, progress is not measured in the slow, painstaking steps of our earthly existence, but in leaps and bounds, propelled by the inner connection we've nurtured here with this divine Universe.

In the dim light of dawn, as the world around me slowly awakened, I sat in meditation and contemplation, seeking connection with the One. Each small revelation, each moment of understanding, felt like a victory. For I knew that these were not just baby steps, but leaps towards a reunion with the Creator, a reunion that universe.

There's no doubt in my mind that God is real. We are like fish in a fish bowl and God is the water. There is nowhere He is not. So why crave? But we remain thirsty. Quench your thirst. Jesus asked a woman for drink by the well, but he could have given her the water of life to never thirst again. What have I been saying? I know where the water of eternal life is that will quench your thirst forever. Do you wish for salvation, then listen and open your mind.

In modern times, we often overlook the things we do in life, the choices we make, that have long lasting effects on our spiritual progress. And yet this progress profoundly affects us. Each act of kindness, every moment of self-reflection, and every drop of God we collect and every step towards understanding this greater purpose will positively impact our future. You cannot touch the sun, but you can feel its warmth and see the things it illuminates. Spiritual wealth is not a myth. It is as real as the sun and its warmth.

Some may find these concepts unconvincing, primarily because they don't align with their current beliefs. Others may dismiss the idea of life after death as unscientific or the product of fanciful imagination. But what if it isn't?

One who chooses to ignore the possibility of gaining spiritual wealth in this life closes the door to a vast realm of potential understanding and growth. What if that inner sun of Truth could be felt and your mind could be illuminated?

For those who are ready to choose to open their minds to the possibility of a continued existence beyond the physical realm, I am here to tell you the secret key to unlock that door rests within you as God Himself and the rewards will have lasting effects both here and here after.

Like the analogy from the film "The Matrix," the choice between the red pill and the blue pill is emblematic of the decision we face when considering the possibility of self-discovery. The red pill represents the willingness to embrace a deeper, often more challenging reality. The blue pill, on the other hand, symbolizes the choice to remain in blissful ignorance, and remain asleep. But by choosing the blue pill, we deny ourselves the opportunity to wake up.

The choice is only one we can make. The reward is a deeper connection with your higher self and the Universe.

My main takeaway from all these experiences was I began to feel the presence of God on a regular basis whenever I sat for meditation. This presence still grows stronger the longer I stay focused on the Word within. This profound realization arose because of my continued dedication to absorbing this divine energy and acquiring more spiritual wealth. Although these concepts may be new to you, God isn't some old man in a far off distant place or in some old dusty book only the elite understand. No, I can now feel God's presence within my soul. God doesn't speak to me in words. I have to understand God on His level. God only exists in the present moment. God is within. He isn't a man or woman, nor human, but an energetic life force, a stream of sound and consciousness flowing like a river through out the universe. God exists as energy both within and without and is always present. To Find Him, look within. The original energetic form God takes is the Word of God or inner sound. This sound can be heard and by listening this sound it can be absorbed as energy. I realized this was what I had been missing in order to feel alive. I had finally found the sustenance I'd been searching for within.

All of these experiences will endure like stars in the night sky. And in their light, I found my way. I came to understand the presence of the Divine had never left me.

Like the air I breathe, the source of energy that powers the entire universe also permeates every aspect of my existence and is so close to me that I constantly overlook it. This essential energy underneath all things was also within the very fabric of my own awareness. I didn't need to search far and wide to find God. I only needed to look within. I only needed to be. At last, the wandering of my restless soul ended in the space between my thoughts.

In the olden times, meditation was considered a science. This scientific technique brings about union of soul and God. Modern culture might find this strange or paradoxical. But wisdom from the ancients has survived the test of time. As my teacher's teacher, Sant Kirpal Singh has said, "The path to the One is through oneness." The pathway back to God, asks up to focus on God, and become one with that energetic force that permeates the entire cosmos. This is the Way that will lead you back to eternal life.

My heartfelt thanks and praise goes to all my teachers for their guidance; O dedicate this book to Prem Rawat, Sant Thakar Singh Ji and the current Sant Mat teacher, as well as the teachers Sant Kirpal Singh Ji, Sant Sawan Singh Ji and her Holiness Smt. Chandra Prabha of the Sawan Adhyamtic Satsang Society.

I also want to acknowledge and show my gratitude to the current spiritual head of Kriya Yoga, Paramahansa Prajanada who is the successor of Paramahamsa Hariharanada at whose feet he attained the stage of cosmic unity.

With profound gratitude and appreciation for my teachers, I have retold my story in hopes that it may inspire others to look within for answers, inner peace and maybe help guide or open a path towards an inner awakening.